GLORIA

The autobiography of
Gloria Hunniford

Gloria Hunniford
with Geoffrey Giuliano and
Deborah Lynn Black

ARROW

This edition published by Arrow Books Limited 1994

1 3 5 7 9 10 8 6 4 2

First published in the United Kingdom in 1993 by
Century
Random House UK Ltd, 20 Vauxhall Bridge Road, London SW1V 2SA

Arrow Books Ltd
Random House UK Ltd, 20 Vauxhall Bridge Road, London SW1V 2SA

Random House Australia (Pty) Limited
20 Alfred Street, Milsons Point, Sydney,
New South Wales 2061, Australia

Random House New Zealand Limited
18 Poland Road, Glenfield
Auckland 10, New Zealand

Random House South Africa (Pty) Limited
PO Box 337, Bergvlei, South Africa

Random House UK Limited Reg. No. 954009

A CIP catalogue record for this book
is available from the British Library

ISBN 0 09 922031 8

Printed and bound in Great Britain by
Cox & Wyman Ltd, Reading, Berkshire

Contents

Soda Farls and Hooleys

No matter how hard or how long I looked I could never work out how he did it. I could feel my eyes swell to the size of the saucers as, with hands never still for a moment, he wove a pattern in the air above me. Coloured streamers, wands, Chinese rings, magic boxes and bouquets of paper flowers flew around my head, then vanished as suddenly as they'd appeared. Hands still weaving, he'd pluck a gold coin from my ear, then pull a dove out of nowhere. Finally, with a flourish, he'd put twelve razor blades in his mouth, followed by a little ball of cotton; when he pulled the cotton out again it would be unravelled and the razor blades would be threaded all along it.

'You realise, there aren't any female magicians?' I once pointed out. 'Maybe one day I could take over?'

'You aren't fooling your old Dad, Gloria,' he said. 'You just want to find out how I do the razor blade trick – I know what you're up to.'

We were a family of amateur entertainers, and I was

named after Gloria Swanson, the screen vamp whom my father adored. In the movies Glorias were conniving vixens, molls, bad girls. I hated my name. I didn't want to rebel, didn't want to be difficult even. All my attempts at deception were completely transparent, just like my attempt at finding out how to do my father's tricks. I'm a conformist. I want to belong.

When I look back at my childhood I see a good place to belong to. In fact more than a good place, it was magical – a small-town kind of magic that an outsider might easily miss, but magic nevertheless. It was a time and place strong in thought and feeling, a time of family life centred around the kitchen table, of home baking and homespun entertainment, of honour, honesty, 'saving yourself' for marriage and hard work. Today's more sophisticated children might find these values impossibly, unbelievably innocent, but I recall them now because they have stayed with me and helped me through the bad times.

I was born in my parents' front bedroom on 10 April, 1940, a major disappointment to my sister Lena, on whose birthday I made my grand entrance. I wasn't exactly the present she had in mind. Apparently she took one peek at my scrawny red face and howled, 'But I wanted a puppy!'

There were eventually five of us sharing the terraced house – two-up, two-down and an outside loo – at 94 Armagh Road, Portadown, a small market town in semi-rural Northern Ireland. I shared a bed with my sister, while my brother, Charles, was in with our parents. I remember the five of us crammed round the kitchen table. There was always a full pot of tea on it and I remember butter oozing through hot bread just out of the oven and the thick-spread jam Mum made from strawberries and raspberries from the garden. When I think of childhood it's those wonderful kitchen smells which evoke so many memories. Half our garden was taken up by a loft containing about fifty pigeons. Dad had kept homing pigeons since he was a lad. I remember their warm, faintly disgusting smell and the beautiful colours of their wings in sunlight – how I used to dream of all the far-off places they'd fly to on their races! And I remember, too, the lone dove my Dad used in his magic tricks. I have a half memory that it used to talk, but, no, that can't be right – it would never have got a word in edgeways anyway.

I was born with a tongue-tie, a small abnormality, a restrictive piece of skin under the tongue. I was taken to the doctor, who snipped it with a special pair of silver scissors, and after that, well, let's just say that in a family of champion talkers I held my own. My Mum later said, 'I sometimes wonder if we did the right thing!' Mind you, she did her fair share of chatting round that black range in the kitchen. I remember night after night an array of neighbours and friends, chatting about everything under the sun – difficulties with children, new knitting patterns, the latest style, days out. While all of this was going on it was the clicking of the knitting needles to the clacking of their tongues.

Perhaps because I was brought up surrounded by so much happy talk, I never really liked being on my own. In fact one of my earliest memories is of sitting crying on the stairs, because for the first time everyone else had gone out and left me by myself. Silence petrified me.

The best storyteller I've ever heard and the person I most wanted to talk to and be with was my father, Charlie. He was a self-taught man. He had left school at thirteen, and he worked as an advertising manager on the local newspaper. He sold the space, wrote the witty slogan, designed the advert, drew the picture if needs be – everything. He gave one hundred per cent to the job in a way you don't often find these days. I remember him turning down a bonus, even though we could have done with the money. It was a question of stubborn pride. He said to his boss: 'If you think I'm doing a good job, give me a higher salary.'

At home he could turn his hand to anything: not just D.I.Y. round the house, but painting, framing pictures, making dolls' furniture. He even taught me how to knit! Mum's patience wouldn't stretch that far, so she taught him, and he taught me. Birthday and Christmas cards always came with an original Charles Hunniford poem – despite his lack of education he had a wonderful turn of phrase. He was full of surprises. I remember one Christmas he went to the trouble of rigging up a life-sized dummy of a man which he positioned on the stairway. He fed a cord through the dummy's body which led up to the bedroom. Then at 5:00 am when he heard our feet creaking at the top of the stairs he pulled the cord, making this fella's arm move and sending us scampering back to the safety of our beds. My parents always made Christmas special. The morning turned into a treasure hunt – I'd find a bicycle behind a couch, a doll on top of a curtain rod or slippers inside the cupboard.

Getting a bicycle for Christmas was all-important because we were a cycling family. Portadown is surrounded by beautiful countryside famous for its Bramley apple orchards. We didn't own a car. We didn't need one. It was a small world, everything within walking or cycling distance. Dad taught me to ride a bike, putting me on it, pushing it, then cycling ahead on his own bike to catch me. From then on trips into the country involved a column of four bikes, with my brother tied on to a cushion on my father's handlebars. What innocent, blissful days!

Travelling always appealed to Dad. It was part of his zest for continually finding new things. It seems poignant to me now that he used to fantasise about Alan Whicker's job. 'Look at the travel you'd get, the people you'd meet. A journalist, that's the job for me,' he'd say wistfully, 'a globe-trotting interviewer.' He even looked a bit like Alan Whicker with his glasses, suave moustache and gently greying hair.

The only time I can remember cheating at school was when Dad wrote an essay for my English class. Focused on a tiny country cottage, it was so sparkling I simply re-cycled it throughout my school years, plugging in a few new details to fit the set topic; whether it was supposed to be about a train ride or a picnic, it always seemed to end up at that sunny little cottage with roses round the door. This was Dad's and my little secret.

My most treasured memory of my Dad, though, is of stopping by his office on a Saturday morning, hoping he'd take me to Bacci's ice-cream parlour for a dish of crushed pineapple ice-cream. The taste was heavenly, but more important than that was having Dad all to myself.

It wouldn't be fair to say my parents had favourites, but Mum and Lena were very close for the first seven years, and then, I suspect, Dad claimed me until Charles was born – as the baby he became everyone's favourite with his angelic face and shock of blond curls. At night Dad would go and lie down beside him to help him get to sleep. But none of this should be taken as saying Dad was soft on me or on any of us. He was a disciplinarian of the old school and master of the house. His word was law.

I was tempted, as all children are, by the fire on the stove. 'Don't touch that range,' he'd warn, but I'd linger a bit too close, thinking about it. Finally he held my finger on the edge of it for a searing few seconds in order to teach me a hard lesson. Believe me, I never touched the stove again.

I remember getting upset whenever my sister was being punished. 'Don't hit her!' I'd scream, and then I'd end up getting the smacking intended for Lena.

On another occasion I was playing by Dad's pigeon loft, the steps of which were slippery from rain. 'Gloria, now don't climb those stairs, you'll fall.' But of course I did anyway, and promptly went crashing down the steps. I ran in crying, but instead of comforting me, he gave me a good wallop across the legs.

There were certain kinds of behaviour he wouldn't tolerate around the house.

'Oh frig!' I said one day.

'Sorry?' he said.

'Oh frig!' I said.

'Out!' he said, pointing in the direction of the front door. There was an icy look in his eyes I hadn't seen before.

'But why?' I protested innocently. 'I don't understand.'

'We don't use that kind of language in this house. Now get out!'

My mother intervened. I'd just had a bath and my hair was still dripping wet. 'You can't send her out, Charlie. It's turning cold and she'll catch pneumonia.'

'Out, out, OUT!'

I had to take refuge with a neighbour. I waited until my mother came and smuggled me back inside and up to my bedroom.

My mother, May, was one of the kindest people in the world, always the peacemaker. 'It doesn't matter,' she'd say, in a gentle but slightly exasperated voice whenever she sensed a row brewing round the kitchen table. Mum was a lovely, cuddly woman with a warm smile and a ready laugh. If Dad was the enthusiast flitting from one project to the next, Mum was more down to earth. One of her favourite sayings was 'All you need in life is a bed and a good pair of shoes, because if you're not in one, you're in the other.' The kitchen was her domain, and I always remember her being there, always ready with a cup of tea. 'A full pot's just as easy as a quarter', Mum would say. The kitchen was also where the radio was, where we listened to 'Take your Pick', 'Workers' Playtime' or 'Variety Bandbox'. I'd settle there with my *Rupert* or *Girl's Own* annuals, or my favourite book, *Little Women*.

Every day I'd pedal home from school for lunch to be met by the aroma of home-made soup or hot stew. There might be food from the garden; potatoes, lettuce, spring onions, parsley, or some of that wonderful jam. Every week Mum would make nine different kinds of bread, including treacle-bread, tea cake, wheaten and soda farls, which were shaped into small triangles and fired on the griddle. She baked so much, she often ended up giving half of it away – no wonder she was popular with the neighbours. We always had to have cooked breakfasts to set us up for the day, 'Ulster fry-ups' – soda farls with bacon, eggs and potato bread.

The only time I can remember Mum being less than calm and reasonable was during thunderstorms. She had a completely *un*reasonable fear of them – a phobia, I suppose you might call it these days. 'Get away from the window!' she'd warn us. 'Don't let the lightning hit you!'

She unhooked every plug in the house, thinking it might come to get us through the electricity sockets, and she would shoo us under the kitchen table or into the cubbyhole under the stairs. There she would sit, hugging her brood to her.

There is no doubt in my mind that May Hunniford relished her role as wife and homemaker. No one could have been a better mother. But did she ever yearn for anything more, for wider horizons than those represented by those four kitchen walls? Possibly, for the only row I can ever remember my parents having was over a job my mother wanted to work in a bakery that cousin Evelyn was opening.

'No wife of mine is going out to work!' said Dad. Mum just sat there.

'Why don't you ever stand up for yourself?' I demanded.

In her usual style, she said, 'In the end what does it matter?'

In many ways Dad was the typical working-class domineering head of the household – and Irish men have probably always been extreme examples of this type. Dad would never have been caught cooking or shopping or taking the children out in the pram, and if, for example, Mum wanted to go out to the Mothers' Union, she could go if it suited him to babysit. Ridiculous? Perhaps, but Dad took full and ultimate responsibility for the running of the household – the buck always stopped with him. Maybe Mum would have enjoyed more freedom, but on reflection I believe she always seemed happy with her lot.

Mum came from quite a well-off farming background. She used to tell us stories about her mother taking her shopping in Elliot and Stevenson's, a Portadown couturier so upmarket our neighbours said they couldn't afford to window-shop there. I still have photos of her as a young woman, slim and elegant in pointed lace collars. Right until she died she took great pride in her appearance. I know my love of clothes comes from her.

Granny McCann was an imposing figure, statuesque in her satins and pearls. She had the air of one accustomed to fine things – she wore ruby and diamond rings – and I remember she had a collection of beautiful ruby glass and fine pieces of furniture. I think perhaps Mum was always just a bit frightened of her; she kept the fact that she smoked secret from her mother even into middle age, worried she'd think it not quite respectable.

My grandmother visited us in town every Saturday come what may, and my lasting memory is of her sitting by the window in the parlour, watching everyone go by. Because she lived deep in the country she expected us to know every single person, much to my mother's frustration; Granny lived on a farm at the end of a meandering country lane, so everybody who passed by her door had a reason for being there.

I have no recollection of my grandfather, who died before I was born. But Granny continued to live in that rambling old farmhouse, a short four-mile cycle ride away. We used to visit her a couple of times a week – families were more closely knit then. As children we used to love going over there. She kept a donkey in the orchard, and we used to give him a hard time when we played Cowboys and Indians out on the range.

The highlight of the summer was the haymaking season, when the sun always seemed to be shining. The long grass had to be cut and allowed to dry. Huge pitchforks were used to toss the hay, and eventually it was made into haystacks. To my dying day I'll remember the image of Granny making her way through the hayfield, carrying that huge double-lidded wicker basket, lined with red and white gingham, and containing the most mouth-watering goodies straight from the oven – butter dripping from hot bread and icing melting down those fairy cakes. After all that work, we relished those farm mugs of steaming tea poured from the enormous farmhouse teapot, and we didn't mind the odd fly or two.

Probably the ultimate excitement was when the time came to move the haystacks into the hayloft for the winter. Uncle Geordie would drive the tractor which pulled the hay-shift, and once the stack was loaded we'd jump on the end for a ride back to the farm.

The great stone-flagged kitchen had an Irish pine dresser and an inglenook fireplace so big that we could stand in it and look straight up and see the sky. A cast-iron crane-like contraption swung over the flames of the fire, and from it hung this huge black cauldron. If it wasn't bubbling with soup or stew for the family it was cooking up potato skins or other slops for the pigs. Come the evening, oil lamps and candles would provide what little light was needed. The conversation was slightly quieter and more genteel than in our own home. When one of the neighbours, Jack, came in he'd sit right at the back of the kitchen, and I've never seen a man with such a good aim. When he'd decided he'd chewed his tobacco enough, that spit never missed the fire. We just had to make sure we never got in the way.

If we were staying the night, when bedtime came I always made Granny come with me to the end room. I was afraid of the shadows created by the single oil lamp as we passed by the room where the big old butter churn sat and the room where big sacks of baking flour and wheaten meal were kept. What a relief it was finally to climb up into that huge bed with its antique brass ends and crawl under that soft feather eiderdown.

My recurring dream is not of the bed or the shadows, but of Selshion Moss, across the road from the farm. The Moss is where the turf was cut to burn on the fire. We used to play there among the wild flowers. My dream is that I'm digging in the Moss, and the more I dig, the more coins I find.

One day I came from school, and straightaway I knew something was wrong. Granny had died of a stroke that morning. It was my first brush with death, and something I didn't really understand. Mum was always such a sunny person – I felt desolate seeing her face crumpled with pain. She cried for days – and we cried for her as much as for Granny. Lena and I made her endless cups of tea, while Dad prepared the hot whiskey toddies which he thought were the perfect antidote to sickness, nerves, births and even deaths.

Irish wakes and funerals in that part of the country often had the coffin propped up in the corner of the room. There was a lot of singing and dancing. Although that didn't happen with Granny, there was a bit of a hooley in the farmhouse kitchen. Because it was the first time I'd experienced death, I couldn't understand all her friends and family sitting around feeding their faces and cracking jokes. I wanted to scream at them to go home.

It was traditional that everybody in turn had to look at the corpse to pay their last respects, which in this case was laid out in the bedroom. When it came to my turn, I clung to Lena's hand. She led me upstairs by candlelight to the bedroom, and we approached the great four-poster bed.

'Doesn't she look good?' she said.

When I finally opened my eyes I saw that she did.

2

Grass Soup and Tied Swings

When Roger Bannister broke the four-minute mile record, I remember thinking, with my childish logic, that from now on it would take me only eight minutes to walk the two miles to school.

I'll never forget my teacher at Church Street Primary, Mrs Forsythe. You'd rush through the door so as not to be late, eyes still blurred with sleep, and even before you'd sat down she'd be hurling a barrage of times tables questions in your face. 'Six fives? Two fours? Seven nines?' If you didn't snap the answer right back, she'd toss you over her knee and spank you. Happily I'd been well prepared for all this by my sister Lena.

Lena – short for Helena – was seven years older than me, and my brother, Charles, was seven years younger: it seemed the spirit only moved our parents once every seven years. The spacing meant that we were guardians for each other rather than true companions. (It was only when we were all married that we seemed to have anything in common.) Lena would moan if Mum said I had to tag along with her, and so would I if I had to take Charles when I went to play with my friends. 'Gloria, you come back here and get your brother this instant!' my mother would shout out of the back door as I tried to escape down the alley to the tree-house at the end of the road, or to the rowing boats on the river Bann.

Lena's dream was to become a schoolteacher – her pride and joy was her birthday present of blackboard, easel and cane – and who better to practise on than her little sister? Especially since she was *forced* to put up with my company. So every Saturday without fail she held classes for me, even setting me homework for the following week, and if I gave her trouble she'd rap me over the knuckles with the cane. The good side of all this was that I could read and write before I went to primary school, which saved me many a smack from Mrs Forsythe. Years later Lena boasted: 'Don't you think I did a good job?'

If I was a nuisance to my sister she held the ace trick up her sleeve. The Cull family up the road had a caravan in their back garden that they used on holidays. Joan Cull was a friend of Lena's, and they used to spend hours playing house inside and around the caravan. If Lena was forced to take me along, she'd mix clumps of grass with water and make me drink it.

In those days the church was our social life. On Saturday nights there were the 'socials' in the church hall, where we'd play parlour games or dance the hokey cokey or the military two-step. On Sundays we'd go to church five times: junior service and choir practice at 10:00, senior service at 11:00, Sunday school at 2:00, the main service at 7:00, followed by a prayer meeting of the Christian Workers' Union. It's easy to forget what a hold the Church had on every tiny aspect of our lives then, down to the swings on the recreation ground being tied up on Sundays; it was even frowned upon to mow the lawn. We were raised with unbending notions of right and wrong – compromise was unthinkable. We were Christian soldiers who lived by the Ten Commandments, and even just thinking about deviating in any way carried a very heavy burden of guilt.

The Church of Ireland service is very strict and ritualistic, with a lot of 'up and down' as we would call it: readings, psalms, hymns and prayers and of course 'the sermon'. So every six weeks or so, I couldn't believe my luck when Dad would take me to the Salvation Army Hall in Portadown. I never failed to be amazed that people enjoyed themselves in church so much – tambourines, clapping, smiling, singing, happy faces. That environment started off a healthy respect in my mind for the Salvation Army, topped up by great memories of Christmas morning when they would be under the window playing their carols.

On Radio 2, on the last working day before Christmas I am thrilled to say that we switch our programme from the tiny studio to the large concert hall at Broadcasting House. The public join us there, along with star names, and we very much enjoy the fellowship of the Chalk Farm Band of the Salvation Army. It's always a great occasion to celebrate the season, and sets the tone for Christmas.

As children in Portadown we grew up to understand the difference between Roman Catholics and Protestants. We lived one end of town – they lived the other. They went to their schools, we went to ours. As a Church of Ireland Protestant I was not encouraged to get involved with too many Catholics – certainly not when it came to going out with boys. I realised that one long hot summer when,

as teenagers, my pal Pat Farrell and I were excitedly playing tennis in our local park with some trainee priests.
There was a certain taboo on different levels. They were
off bounds; we also thought them to be very good-looking
and considered it a waste that they were going into the
Church and would never really have an interest in girls. I
got a good ticking off later by my mother for 'gallivanting
around with priests'.

When you met someone new, it was easy to find out
which side they came from. If they went to certain schools
or if they were called Dominic or Sean they were bound to
be Catholic, but I never could get to grips with the old
housewife's tale – 'you can tell a Catholic because their
eyes are too close together'. Understandably, though,
your religion was always near the top of the list, particularly when it came to jobs.

After names and addresses, the next question on the
application form was religion. This determined whether
or not a company would take you on, and, of course this
type of discrimination ultimately became a great scoring
point in the civil rights movement led by Bernadette Dev-
lin in 1969. As we all know, ancestral conflicts do not settle
easily and some say that Northern Ireland is paying a con-
tinuing high price for the absence of political initiative – a
good example was the failure of the all-party talks
amongst the local parties a couple of years ago. I am obviously not a political commentator, but at the root of
everything, and without trying to be too simplistic in the
middle of a very complicated situation, I believe one of the
ways of getting rid of the bigotry and segregation is to
integrate children at primary school level – after all,
children weren't born bigots. In fact, a few very successful schemes have been carved out at forward-looking

schools, where Catholic and Protestant sit side by side; each has his or her own religious training and they grow up with a healthy respect for each other – as indeed happens in other countries.

Although that was unheard of in my primary school days I was also very aware that my Dad had many Catholic friends, for example in the Edgarstown Pigeon Club, where he was one of the leading lights. Also there were few barriers when it came to sport or entertainment. For instance, there were a couple of Catholics from the South in our concert party, but we were always amused when they had to play the British National Anthem at the end of the show. Some of these venues were staunchly Protestant, like the Orange Halls, and they would not have taken kindly to discovering Catholics in our midst.

As a child I always thought that the 12 July parades were a bit barbaric. The loyalists who belonged to the Orange Lodges would parade behind their pipe and brass bands every year, celebrating the victory of the English King, William of Orange, in the Battle of the Boyne in 1690. To this day 12 July is an official holiday – in fact most people take the 12 July fortnight as their annual holidays.

The effigy of the traitor Billy Lundy would be burnt on every street corner on the night of 11 July. In the weeks leading up to the big night, children would collect, beg or steal any piece of wood or cardboard box they could find, and the pride was to have the biggest bonfire. Some of them would rise thirty feet high, and balancing precariously on top would be the life-size dummy of Billy Lundy. As night fell, the sky over the town would be lit up by dozens of crackling fires spitting out hundreds of sparks, while the local people sang the traditional songs and danced amongst the embers. Although it was always a ritual that we toured the bonfires, as a child it was something I viewed with a mixture of fright and excitement. The next morning, as the bonfires still smouldered, the Orangemen would get ready to march.

Our house was a hive of activity – Dad's distinctive orange sash was taken out of the tissue from the year before and duly ironed for the big day. Complete with black bowler hat and best suit, it was topped off with a tightly rolled plastic mac ready for the rain which never seemed to be far away. The streets were festooned with red, white and blue bunting and our front garden in Armagh Road had a huge Union Jack flag displayed, with 'God Save the Queen' placards standing in the rockery. While Dad marched, the rest of the family took our places on the route waving our little flags and listening to the almost tribal sound of the beat of the huge Lambeg drums, alongside the flute and pipe bands. It was in these marching bands that many musicians got valuable experience, none more so than the now world-renowned flautist James Galway.

My paternal grandfather had fought in the trenches in the First World War. I was mesmerized by his rows of shining medals as he marched every year on Armistice Day with the ex-servicemen's lodge. Granny Hunniford had had a tough life. She'd worked as a seamstress in a factory to make ends meet – she'd had six children to support. By the time I knew her she was a frail, sweet-natured old lady with her white hair pulled back in a bun.

They lived a ten-minute walk from our house at No. 14 Alexander Gardens, with a monkey puzzle tree in the garden. The whole of the living room seemed to be taken up with the twisted bulbous legs of the table which Granny obviously spent ages polishing. Every Sunday night we congregated around the table, the main entertainment being whist. As a child I'd spend hours watching over my father's shoulder as he played his trump cards. It was a thrill to be finally accepted and allowed to play a hand. The game went on all evening, and during the proceedings the women would go off to cook supper (the 'fourth meal' in Ireland).

I remember one Christmas Eve spent there. Everyone gathered round an enormous Christmas tree that took up the only remaining space. Granny Hunniford had a special gift for each of the children. I had a doll with glossy, wavy hair, a beautiful white satin dress covered in sequins and a wand trimmed with silver brocade and glitter. As we walked home that night, there was a heavy snowfall. Dad broke off a huge fir tree branch, glittering with frost. When we got home, he planted it in a pot, clipped on candles and lit them as we got ready for bed.

When I got my eleven-plus, I fiercely wanted to go to grammar school.

'Absolutely not,' said Dad. 'You don't want to go to university, do you? You don't want to be a doctor or a lawyer? Look at Lena. She's done very well for herself as a legal secretary.'

'But I want to go to Grammar School. All my friends will be there.'

'Well, you're not going. Anyway, we can't afford the uniform.'

'But I'll help pay – I've got money saved.' After a campaign of foot stomping and stony silences I finally wore them down, and so for the next four years I attended Portadown College. I loved it, history, geography, literature and French all opening up to me. I used to pore over my French texts as if they were storybooks, and I'd read them out to my parents in the kitchen after dinner. Goodness knows what they thought, but I do remember that phrase 'high falutin' nonsense' alongside a sense of pride.

And then there were other, extra-curricular activities. Every lunch hour I'd tear home on my bike, gulp down my poor mother's lovingly prepared pies and tarts, then it was back off to school again to catch the half hour or so left of the ballroom dancing classes held by Mr Spaulding, the Latin teacher, in the assembly hall. Boys would line up on one side, girls on the other, then we'd learn the samba, foxtrot, tango and waltz. I don't know if he ever had 'Come Dancing' ambitions, but in the ensuing years we were to bless him for the social skills he taught us.

In my early childhood movies came into my life in a big way. Each of the three cinemas in Portadown changed programmes three times a week. That's a lot of moviegoing. Alexander Walker, the famous film critic, lived in our town, and has a lot to thank the Savoy, Summerson's and the Regal picture houses for. I'd sit at the front, dreaming of being June Allyson to Jimmy Stewart's Glenn Miller or Leslie Caron in *An American in Paris*. And which girl has ever been able to resist identifying with Vivien Leigh in *Gone with the Wind*? Saturday mornings were particularly special, because then we had the full works: the ads, Pathé news, the big picture, the wee picture and a diet of Roy Rogers and Gene Autry. Circus epics were a great favourite too, and afterwards my friends and I would re-enact the daring trapeze acts on ropes hung from two sturdy hooks in our back garden. Historical romances were also a big inspiration. I was disappointed that, because of my close-cropped hair, I was always cast in the supporting role of handmaid to my best friend's princess. 'But I want to be the princess this time!'

'No, Gloria. You haven't got any long hair to brush.'

It was about this time that I had my first boyfriend, Dennis, who, I'm afraid, was something of a tightwad. I'd agree to go to the pictures with him, but then he'd say, 'I'll meet you inside', so he didn't have to pay. He might make up for it in the back row by sharing his dolly mixtures, but things came to a head when he went on holiday. He said he'd bring me back a present, so I asked him for a pair of rollerskates. Hardly within the budget of a ten-year-old, you might think, but aim high, I figured. When he brought me back a bottle of eau de cologne I was singularly unimpressed. No more back rows and dolly mixtures for me.

Then there was Robert. He carved me a little wooden heart in secret during woodwork lessons. I didn't fancy him all that much, but I kept the heart anyway.

When I was eight or nine I came home one day from school to find the most elegant, distinguished gentleman I'd ever seen sitting in our parlour – never used except for very special occasions. He was tall and lean with waves of flowing white hair.

'Who's that?' I nudged Mum.

'Gloria, say hello to your great uncle Jim from Canada.'

I hadn't the faintest idea where Canada was, but I listened excitedly as Uncle Jim told of his adventures on leaving Ireland as a boy of nineteen, and sailing across the ocean to a foreign land. He spoke of towering mountains, limitless prairies, Indians and Eskimos, and of the sheer size of the country – so big that you could fit the whole of Ireland into Lake Superior with room left over. Over the years he had built up his own electrical contracting business which had done fabulously well. He opened his bag and out poured wonderful smelling fruits, nuts and all kinds of sweets. In a Northern Ireland still under post-war rationing this was big news, and from that moment he represented the land of milk and honey.

That Sunday he took me to a Quaker meeting – my mother's was an old Quaker family, though she herself had given up going to meetings after she married my father. I watched with fascination as the congregation sat completely silent until quite suddenly someone would rise to his or her feet and deliver a spirit-moved prayer, song or passage from scripture. Uncle Jim whispered, 'Why don't you sing?'

'But I need an introduction,' I said, panicking.

'It doesn't work that way here,' he smiled. 'When there's a silence you just do whatever moves you.'

Finally I mustered the courage to stand and sing a hymn I'd learned in Sunday school. Then I sang a few more – I caught Uncle Jim's eye and delighted in him sitting there beaming proudly.

As the end of his holiday approached, I heard him talking to my mother: 'You know Gloria has great potential, May. Why don't you let her come back to Canada with me? I'll educate her – I promise she'll have all the very best opportunities.'

No Irish mum was about to let her young daughter go any further than the immediate neighbourhood, and the matter was dropped. I ran off to my room, throwing myself on to the bed in tears – as a child I had no concept of what it really meant. How could she do this to me? I thought. Didn't she know she was ruining my life?

It wasn't long afterwards that Portadown was suddenly blitzed by an invading army of American evangelists, led by Billy Graham. My friends and I were caught up in a whirlwind of colourful revival tents, rousing gospel songs and charismatic preachers delivering their message in a hypnotic American drawl. I'll never forget that first revival meeting. The local Presbyterian church was packed with zealous converts, eager hopefuls and a few sceptical curiosity seekers like ourselves. Then out strode a commanding figure in a crackling new black suit, all confidence and bravado. I was instantly mesmerised by his booming voice and his message of hope, mercy and forgiveness – so much more uplifting, on the face of it, than the message of guilt we'd been brought up on . . .

Then came the call to accept the Lord as your personal saviour before all your friends and neighbours. 'Come forward,' said the preacher. 'Cleanse your souls, wash yourselves in the blood of the Lamb.' I felt myself rising, walking forward, my feet scarcely seeming to touch the ground. I was pulled towards the front of the church, till in one exhilarating moment I was born again, aglow with new sensations.

Back at home Mum and Dad listened quietly and with no apparent signs of panic. 'Fine, if that's what you want,' said Mum. 'Just as long as you realise what you're doing.'

I took a deep breath. 'Of course, you know I can't sing any more.'

'Why not?' said Dad.

'I couldn't possibly carry on going to public entertainments.'

My parents didn't push the issue, and the next two years of my life became a continuous round of prayer meetings and bible study. Gone were the dancing and the movies, because these were dreadfully sinful. I must have been completely unbearable.

Little by little, though, I began to notice things. I discovered, for example, that some of my fundamentalist friends had been stealing away to the pictures in Belfast. Apparently movie-going was a sin in Portadown but not far away and out of sight in the big city.

And then Dad said: 'Don't you think God gave you your voice to sing with?'

Of course, as in everything else, he was absolutely right.

3

Keeping Dick at the Daffodil Teas

We had one of those oversized Bakelite wirelesses which sat on the kitchen shelf. At an early age I reasoned that if I could hear them, then they would be able to hear me, so I would stand on a chair and spend hours singing into the front of it, waiting and yearning to be discovered.

My parents had sent me to the local music teacher, who'd tried to make me do scales and the standard classical pieces, but I'd have none of it – all I wanted were the pop songs of the day. I knew I could sing.

'It's no use, Mr Hunniford,' said the teacher. 'You're wasting your money, she'll never buckle down.' She was right. I was too impatient to get up before a live audience. I was waiting to be discovered.

Dad would perform his magic tricks several nights a week as part of a travelling show called the Mid-Ulster Variety Group. This wandering troupe of modern-day troubadours performed at schools, church halls and village halls from one end of the country to the other. In the days before TV they were wildly popular, great evenings of homespun entertainment.

Singers, dancers, comedians and other variety acts would parade into a village, then set up in the biggest meeting place. If there was a proper stage all well and good; if not a makeshift stage would be constructed out of trestle tables. Sometimes the hall wouldn't have a piano and one had to be found and hauled there from some house in the village by a few burly men. More trestle tables were set up in lines up and down the hall, and teas were served on them before the performance began – gallons of tea in great silver urns, sandwiches, scones, cakes and apple tart. But what really made the trestle tables groan were the hundreds upon hundreds of daffodils that decorated then – which is why in springtime these do's were known as Daffodil Teas.

When the daffodils weren't in season they were called Meat Suppers. These were proper sit-down knife-and-fork dinners, lit by tilly lamps, where Irish stew would be served, or salads with slices of ham which were so thin you could see the pattern of the plate through them.

Well no doubt the food *was* sometimes meagre, the jokes a little well-worn and some of the entertainment terribly amateur by today's standards – it was not unknown, for example, for the trestle tables to collapse with the weight of the performers on top of them – but however it went the people laughed and cheered, sometimes till the tears ran down their cheeks. My country so often presents a grim face to the world, I wish I could recreate some of the innocence of the Daffodil Teas and Meat Suppers. They were the most good-natured occasions I ever expect to enjoy, the very picture of good- and open-heartedness.

And to a child, of course, they couldn't have been more glamorous.

So almost from the moment I could speak I begged my father to take me along. He let me watch from the wings, bedazzled by the beautiful women in their sequins and the lovingly polished musical instruments. A typical bill would start with the compere, George Nixon, introducing the troupe. We all sang the opening song, 'Happy Days Are Here Again'. Then there would be a fiddle player or accordionist (the accordionist, I remember, was called Joe McVeigh), followed by some slapstick comedy – perhaps with the old hot water bottle down the trousers joke – then two sisters tap-dancing to 'The Lullaby of Broadway', a recitation – 'Albert and the Lion', perhaps – a tenor, a comic and, top of the bill, Ken and Eddy Bush, the bell-ringers, and for a touch of class schoolteacher McKay Kenny would read from the great poets.

But top of the bill for me was always my father in his top hat and tails, performing the sleights of hand I still hadn't managed to figure out, no matter how many hours I'd spent secretly poking round his cupboard of magic tricks while he was out of the house.

I'd been accompanying Dad on the concert party circuit for some months when one night he suddenly asked, 'How would you like to come on stage at the end when we sing the National Anthem?' My little heart thumping, I took to the stage, proudly holding Dad's hand. Being up there, hearing the sound of my voice ringing out above the crowd and then the thunderous (and no doubt over-generous) applause of the audience, I knew I'd found my calling.

All that singing into the Bakelite wireless had paid off. Forget about all that classical rubbish. Saturday mornings I was up bright and early, because that was the day the new sheet music arrived in town. Off to the music shop I would go to hear the pianist plugging the new songs. Then it was off to the house of Gail Sheridan, the concert party pianist, who would painstakingly put me through my paces.

I made my official debut as a member of the Mid-Ulster Variety Group on 9 April, 1949 in Portadown's Cloncore Orange Hall. Dad hoisted me on stage in a yellow taffeta dress, the only sequins we could afford being the few silver ones sprinkled around the neck. My repertoire began with 'Powder Your Face With Sunshine', complete with overblown gestures and a non-stop grin, followed by 'A – You're Adorable' – and I was beginning to feel more at ease with each passing verse. By the time I came to 'Buttons and Bows' I didn't want to get off the stage. A whip round with the hat up and down the rows

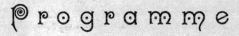

Programme

OPENING CHORUS BY THE COMPANY.

PART I.		PART II	
		INTERVAL (BALLOT)	
1. BOY THOMAS	*Accordeonist*	1. BOY THOMAS	*Accordeonist*
2. EILEEN ANDERSON	*Soprano*	2. EILEEN ANDERSON	*Soprano*
3. E. HERBERT	*Dame Comedian*	3. C. HUNNIFORD	*Conjuror*
4. RUBY MOORE	*Songs & Taps*	4. THE TWO MACS	*Duets*
5. BUSHE BROTHERS	*Bell Ringers*	5. E. HERBERT	*Dame Comedian*
6. J. M'MAHON	*Tenor*	6. GLORIA & RUBY	*Songs*
7. SINTON & HYNES	*Comedians*	7. BUSHE BROTHERS	*Bell Ringers*
8. GLORIA HUNNIFORD	*Child Vocalist*	8. SINTON & HYNES	*Comedians*
9. H. M'CANN	*Baritone*		

CLOSING CHORUS BY THE COMPANY.

of the hall produced seven shillings and sixpence – a fortune for my first fee.

For the next six years I travelled with this wandering troupe. We had to cram into the cars, and I always sat on my Dad's knee in the back of an old Morris 8. He kept a diary of the tricks he performed – he was always inventing new ones – and he encouraged me to keep what I called my Show Work Book. A typical entry reads: 'Lisbellaw, Wednesday, 12 January, 1955. Sang "Happy Wanderer", "This Ole House", "The Little Shoemaker". Wore white petticoats. In luck! Paid fifteen shillings!" Eventually I was making one pound a night, an extraordinary sum for a child in those days.

My Auntie Myrtle made my stage clothes. I used to go down to Mrs McCracken's to ask if I could watch 'Come Dancing' on television – she was the first in the street to have one. It was nothing to do with dancing; I just couldn't believe anybody could have that many sequins on one dress. My aunt was a wizard with the sewing machine. I could show her any cutting from a fashion magazine, I could describe anything I'd seen on 'Come Dancing', and she could make it right down to the starched petticoats. My silver tap shoes were tied with bows and the elastic of my white ankle socks would cling to my legs – in my childish way I tried to look the part.

I became pig-headedly independent with all the money I was earning. I remember coming home one day and telling Mum I needed new socks and vests.

'I'm sorry, Gloria, I can't afford it this week. You'll have to wait.'

'Well then,' I said with an arrogant toss of the head, 'I'm going to buy them myself.'

What an obnoxious little sod!

Sometimes the venues we played were so basic they had no loos, so I had to use the back field, someone coming with me to 'keep Dick'. Then afterwards, with my long satin dress soaking wet from the dew-drenched grass, I'd have to get up on stage in total embarrassment.

Out on the road singing three, four, sometimes five nights a week, often not getting home till 2:00 am, was a hectic schedule by any standards. Mum and Lena were always waiting at the parlour window – I have an image of them peering through a sheen of frost. They'd have a cup of tea ready, then they'd hurry me to bed, waking me up five hours later to go to school.

Mum was very perturbed at those journeys late at night in and around the Border areas of Counties Armagh, Fermanagh and Tyrone. It was the time of the B-Specials in the fifties – an auxiliary group of uniformed men who assisted the Royal Ulster Constabulary, the Northern Ireland police force, to help keep law and order on the Border roads between North and South. When they waved their red-light torches, cars had to stop or they would open fire. I was always scared that our driver wouldn't see the light and we would be shot at. On those dark, lonely roads it was intimidating when the torches were shone into our faces: 'Who are you?' 'Where have you been?' and 'Where are you travelling to?' I was always so relieved when we were sent on our way. The object of the B-Specials was to keep general surveillance in those tricky areas, but also to be on the look out for smuggled goods. You have to remember that those were the post-war years, and because Southern Ireland had been neutral in the Second World War they had no rationing whatsoever.

Entering a sweet shop in the South was like going

into an Aladdin's Cave – no coupons, and all the chocolate and sweets you could carry. I shall never forget the variety of Easter eggs available, and in particular marshmallow ones – my favourite.

While I was busy spending my fee for the night, Dad was concentrating on the more essential foodstuffs like butter, sugar and bacon. This is where his black wooden magic box came into its own. The secret panel which on stage concealed doves, chiffon scarves and card tricks doubled as the perfect hiding-place for smuggled luxuries which would keep our family and indeed the neighbours going for days. Not all of us had a magic box to resort to, but I did find my own unusual hideaway – many a pair of new shoes I smuggled in my knickers.

All this may seem extraordinary by modern standards, but I was having the time of my life. Strangely enough, although I was performing in a semi-professional way those talents didn't seem to spill over into my Portadown College life, even though they had a good drama and music department. Mary Peters, the former Olympic gold medallist, was at the same school, and she often dines out on the story that I beat her in a non-stop talking competition which went on for something like eleven hours – perhaps it was all good training for things to come. The only time I was asked to sing in assembly I performed the Guy Mitchell hit 'She Wears Red Feathers and a Hooly Hooly Skirt' – a weird choice, and no wonder I was never asked to sing in assembly again.

One of my best pals at school was called Ann Downey, and together we went through a phase of reading risqué or 'dirty books' as we called them, thinking this was the height of decadence. *Lady Chatterley's Lover*, I remember, was often plucked out of lockers at break or dinner time so that we could share the naughty pages and the giggles. One afternoon we decided we had to finish the book, so, lying on her sitting room floor with the geography books well spread out as cover, we read every word from cover to cover. However, the best laugh of all was when Ann walked into assembly late the following morning. The book was in her blazer pocket and the title like a belisha beacon poking out at the top of the pocket. Many a Saturday she spent in detention after that!

I remained with the Mid-Ulster Variety Group for a while and then graduated to some outside singing with dance bands. When the singer with Fred Hanna and his show band fell ill, he asked me to fill in at a show at the City Hall, Belfast. Now this was big time. Prior to this I'd only ever gazed at the City Hall through the bus window; it's a very impressive building that dominates the central area of the city. Those magnificent marble staircases and balustrades, the ballroom with its chandeliers – I couldn't believe that I was actually performing in it. I wore a pink strapless ballgown with a tiny waist and a big skirt, and I was paid £16 for two nights' work.

I suppose that nowadays this sort of upbringing wouldn't be allowed by the social workers, but I don't regret a minute of it. On reflection, it was all good training which would stand me in good stead. I learned how to handle myself before an audience, how to judge the sound and timbre of my own voice. More importantly, the work ethic which had always been a part of my childhood was reinforced; I saw that work could be fun, and since then I've always paid my own way. All my life I've almost felt guilty about enjoying work, and it's only recently, when people have suggested that I'm a workaholic, that I've come to realise my whole working life and social life are intermingled – and I love it all so much.

When I was fifteen I got the results of my junior levels, and my singing didn't seem to have done them any harm. As I proudly showed Dad the certificate that proved I'd passed in all fifteen subjects, he said matter-of-factly, 'You're not going on to the senior level, are you?'

'Sure I am,' I quickly replied, sensing trouble.

'What's the point? You've had your four years there. Look, if you go to technical college there's a course for grammar school people where you don't concentrate on the academics but the secretarial skills. That will stand you in very good stead. Look at your sister.'

At that point I knew it was useless to protest. I'd won the battle five years earlier, but this time I could see my parents were resolute. Looking back, I think Dad was simply seeing things from his own very practical stand-point. After all, he'd done what he believed was the best for us, and he'd needed only a very limited education to achieve that.

Yet it was a stinging disappointment. My head-master, a magnetic and inspiring man called Donald Woodman, sent a card protesting. 'You *are* sending her back, aren't you?' he wrote. When my father replied 'We're thinking of sending her to Portadown Technical School for a further two years to study an advanced commercial course, which we believe will suit her temperament', Mr Woodman jumped on his bicycle and pedalled over to our house. I still recall him bursting through the door in his billowing cloak. 'Mr Hunniford,' he exploded, 'I am frankly horrified to learn that Gloria won't be coming back. I just don't believe it. This girl is certainly university material. Why are you saying she can't return?'

'Because she's been at grammar school for four years

now and we think it's time for her to move on to technical college and do other things.'

But this is absurd,' the headmaster protested. 'She could go on to university, she could do anything!'

My father's reply was quiet and resolute: 'Well, I'm sorry, but that's not what we want.'

I knew then it really was over. My school friends commiserated with me as I cried myself stupid. In later years I would realise the irony of it all, how these days parents have to bully their children to do the things I wanted to do so desperately.

At Portadown Technical College I dutifully mastered shorthand, typing and book-keeping, all of which served me well in my later journalistic career. We learned to touch type. What a sight we must have been, twenty-four of us sitting with the typewriter covers over our heads so we wouldn't look at the keys!

If I hadn't been allowed to sing too much at Portadown College, the Tech was different. Suddenly I found myself doing Gilbert and Sullivan, and for some strange reason was cast as the judge in *Trial by Jury*. I stopped the show, not through my singing ability, but because when I was in the middle of 'For I am a judge and a good judge too', in a great flurry of chucking books and papers all over the stage, I unfortunately threw a heavy legal tome at the clerk of the court and knocked him to the floor senseless! Colin Baxter lived to tell the tale.

Life was opening up for me now in many ways. At the age of sixteen or so I started going to dances at the Savoy Ballroom with its glittering mirror balls hanging from the ceiling. The boys would come up to you and say, very formally, 'Would you like to dance?' It was very rude to turn anyone down, so you had to place yourself strategically in the line of vision of anyone you fancied.

My fancy was a dark-haired boy called Desi Allistair. I had fancied him at school for quite some time. He was older than me, a good sportsman, so I had to try to make him notice me. It was only when I went all dolled up to the dance on Saturday night that he began to pay any attention, and of course there was always the 'ladies' choice' to fall back on. Eventually the night arrived when he 'left me home'. What a thrill it was to walk hand-in-hand the one mile to where our house stood on the edge of town. I was an hour and a half late back and we were lingering by the gate. 'Gloria, come in this very second!' yelled my mother in the middle of a long-awaited kiss – I wondered if you really could die of embarrassment, but it was to be the first of many.

None of us had cars in those days. But Desi's father had a brand-new Morris Minor, which we regarded as very posh. In stolen moments Desi taught me to drive. I'll always thank him for his patience. I think I might have married Desi if I hadn't left the country. Still, a quick grope by the gate or in the back seat of the car was as far as it ever went in sexual terms.

In those days I still believed you might get pregnant through your knickers.

One day Andy Trotter, a small wiry man bursting with energy who was manager of the Eagle Star Insurance Company, approached the technical college looking for a fledgling shorthand typist for his busy Portadown branch. So there I was head-hunted at the age of sixteen to work in the office and indirectly be an agent selling car and house insurance.

My workmate was called Margaret Titterington, and

when we got Andy out of the office we had a field day. Fish and chips from the café across the road for lunch, and then the battle to try and get rid of the horrendous stench before the boss would return. What the clients thought about it heaven knows. On sunny days we took it in turn to sit out of the long sash windows in the office to top up our tan, so this office became the mecca for all aspects of life.

Margaret was newly married and very happy to keep an eye on my love life. Desi was always in the background, but a tall, slim young man by the name of Jack McNally got into the habit of calling into our office on a fairly regular basis. It may first of all have been for a motor policy enquiry, but that excuse ran out pretty quickly. Jack and I became enormous pals. Through his family he was to inherit the most beautiful farmhouse and acreage in a village called Richhill in County Armagh, a few miles from Portadown. Coming from a small terraced house it was a rare treat to visit Jack and his family, wandering over the fields and enjoying the sensation of space as Jack carried out some of his farming duties. His mother had a great knack for gardening and I vividly recall her luscious healthy red geraniums trailing around the conservatory. Jack and I used to sit there having a cup of tea, saying that if our relationships didn't work out we would end our days in bath chairs together in the conservatory. Jack eventually married Flo, a girl who made him an extremely capable wife, and I am glad to say they have both remained in that gorgeous house and are very close friends of mine.

The Eagle Star was my first official job – I was trying to become something of a fashion plate now that I was out in the big world of business. Aunt Myrtle's sewing machine was always zinging away with the latest fashions and trends copied out of the glossy magazines which Margaret and I would pore over when we weren't eating fish and chips or selling insurance; but now for the first time, because of my salary, I had enough money to scour the shops in Portadown for the odd mega-treat.

Renee Meneely's, a very upmarket shop, was directly below our office, and a very long-suffering lady used to let this scrawny sixteen-year-old waif try on wonderful silk and satin ball gowns during her lunch break. One day I spotted this fabulous dress with yards and yards of skirt over many net petticoats, and a boned, strapless top with a free-standing frill at the bust line. It had a cream background with wonderful bold splashes of tangerine flowers – striking, dramatic and just the sophistication I thought I needed. Having tried it on each day for a week, I finally decided to 'go for broke'. It took weeks of wages to pay for it, and Myrtle never forgave me for buying from a shop, but it was one of the most memorable dresses I have ever had in my life. It saw me through many teenage 'dos' and singing engagements, and I still have it carefully packed away in its original cardboard box in the roof space. My greatest thrill was that Caron, having always scoffed at my conventional taste, wore it to her first grown-up dance. It was amazing how years of memories came flooding back through a brightly coloured piece of material.

4

The Cheerleader and
the Football Hero

My obsession with going to Canada had grown stronger than ever. Over the years my Uncle Jim's letters were always asking, 'When are you going to come?' In addition, a very close friend in Portadown emigrated there, and on visits home he'd fuel my imagination with his lively descriptions.

When I had enough money saved from the insurance job I finally gathered the courage to confront my parents. 'I'd like to go to Canada,' I told them.

'How long for?' said Mum.

'Maybe six months – or perhaps a year.' I was a young working woman now with her own means and her own mind. Plus, I quickly pointed out, I would be safe in the haven of family.

In the end they gave in on the understanding that I would stay only until Christmas. 'We don't want to get a letter saying you're staying another two months,' said Dad.

Technically speaking I emigrated – in those days it

was known as a ten-pound work passage. I'll never forget that blustery April evening in 1958 when I stood on the deck of the ship that would take me to Liverpool. I had never been outside Ireland, so you can imagine the excitement. But as the boat sailed slowly out of the harbour I saw my father in tears, clutching my brother Charles by the hand. All my grown-up bravado dissolved in that single riveting image. What have I done? I thought. I was sure I'd never see them again.

The boat docked in Liverpool where I was transferred on to the impressive *Empress of Canada*. As if my shattered emotional state weren't enough, my physical condition collapsed too. The rough waters of the Irish Sea sent my stomach reeling and I became wretchedly seasick for two whole days. It was so bad, in fact, that a full third of the crew were similarly laid low. I had wild and totally impractical visions of calling my parents to come and pick me up.

On the third day a crew member whispered to one of my room mates, Janet Barker, 'Listen, if that girl doesn't get up on deck she'll be in that bunk for the rest of the voyage.' Fortunately he was right, and the invigorating sea air along with a firm dose from the ship's doctor soon sorted me out.

Health restored, I began to enjoy the most fabulous time. We soon met a gang of boys from New Zealand and together we romped about the ship, playing all the games, teasing each other and swapping stories. The cuisine was a spread of delicious new foods I'd never tried: lobster stroganoff, luscious deserts such as chocolate mousse and parfait as well as all sorts of exotic fruits like papaya and pomegranate – a far cry from my Mum's soups and stews.

The films in the cinema were all newly released titles – every day was like a Hollywood premiere. In my home town, the films shown in the cinemas were anywhere between several months and several years old. Imagine the thrill of seeing *Gigi* even before most of the world. That musical classic with Louis Jourdain and Leslie Caron has been an all-time favourite of mine ever since.

I turned eighteen on board and the crew celebrated my birthday with a cake, an elaborate party and even presents. I scarcely had time to be homesick with all the attention and fun on board this floating hotel.

It was spring, and ours was the first ship through the St Lawrence river after the icebreaker. So our arrival on the shores of Quebec was breathtaking. We passed massive, towering icebergs, and seals and dolphins frolicked alongside as we slowly made our way down the channel. The ship docked and the whole lot of us set off to explore this incredible walled French city. The winter snow still lingered and the boys from New Zealand had never seen the stuff before. We toured Château Frontenac and strolled the streets of the Old Town among the French speakers as I congratulated myself on understanding some of the language which I had studied back in grammar school. A few of us sauntered accidentally into the 'men only' section of a French restaurant, only to have abuse hurled at us in French by the men, and to be thrown out on our collective feminine ear. After only one intense week of fun and new experiences we all felt like soulmates as we faced this new world.

When we reached Montreal I said goodbye to my comrades and bounded into the waiting arms of Uncle Jim. He couldn't get over how grown-up I was – he'd last seen me as a gangly child. We drove southwest along the

St Lawrence, through Kingston, past Uncle Jim's house on the outskirts, and then to Gannanoque, known as the Gateway to the Thousand Islands. Jim's daughter Beth and her family had built a wonderful house there and he thought it best that I stay with them for a few days to combat the effects of the long journey. They had children close to my age who would help me get my bearings.

Then it all seemed to come apart. The trip had taken its toll; I was suffering from a bad throat infection which had to be treated by Beth's doctor husband. Sick and no longer buoyed by the excitement of the trip, all I wanted was my mother and my own bed. I was 3,000 miles away from home and miserable.

Then came the bombshell. 'We've had a family discussion,' Uncle Jim began, 'and we really feel it would be wrong for you to live with us. We think it best that you stay in the YWCA Youth Hostel in Kingston.'

I felt as if I'd been blindsided by a lorry. 'Gloria,' he explained gently, 'we live in a very remote area with virtually no one your age. You'd have no friends. How would you get work? Whereas, at the hostel you'll have a wonderful and active social life. And, of course, you'll visit us all the time, on weekends and holidays. We'll still do all the things we talked about.'

But I wasn't listening. Had Uncle Jim summoned me across the Atlantic just to stuff me into some boarding house? All those letters over the past decade, telling me about his fabulous home, his family, begging me to come and stay, promising my Mum he'd take care of me. And Mum . . . how would I tell her this? I felt alienated, abandoned and alone. If only I could turn around and run back to Ireland. My life was spiralling out of control.

Ultimately I had no choice but to move into the

YWCA in the hub of Kingston, a bustling university town. I shared a room with a girl named Eleanor Allen, immediately impressing upon her my plight; here I was all the way from the Emerald Isle, 3,000 miles from home. 'Well, I'm 3,500 miles from home and I live in Canada,' she told me. 'Vancouver is on the west coast.'

Shaking off my blues I soon set out job hunting and almost immediately landed a position in the actuarial department of the Empire Life Insurance Company. Heaven only knows what an actuarial department is and to this day I couldn't tell you exactly what the hell I was doing. All I ever seemed to do was call out numbers. One day I remember yelling out 'Eight eighty-eight.'

'What did you say?'

'Eight eighty-eight.'

'Eh girl, we don't know what you're saying, for godsake. What is it you're saying?'

As it turned out my Irish brogue didn't translate well to Canadian-ese. To my co-workers it sounded like 'It-itty-it'. But it was all very good-humoured. This was the first of many cultural adjustments I learned to make. It wasn't the only thing they were confused about, because in their monthly magazine, in saying welcome to the department, they wrote: 'Gloria must hail from a very small village – the other day she got lost on the way to work and almost didn't get here. She lives about four blocks from the office!'

Canada was indeed a brave new world for a young girl from a small town with even smaller horizons. Suddenly I was living alongside Germans, Czechs, Irish and Poles, all working and socialising harmoniously together. Catholic or Protestant, no one asked your religion – it didn't matter.

I was being introduced to new things all the time. Uncle Jim had been right. Living at the hostel, for instance, was like being in a college hall with parties and late-night gossiping with the girls, usually talking about the boys.

After a few weeks I was brain-dead from reading out numbers. Then I ran across an ad in the paper for a job as an accountant's assistant at Old Fort Henry, a major tourist attraction in town. 'You don't have a chance,' warned my uncle. 'You've not enough experience.'

Undaunted, I applied for and landed the position as one of twenty full-time office staff. Within a matter of days the Ontario–St Lawrence Development Commission wrote confirming my appointment as Clerk 2 – at a salary of $230 per month; remembering that I had landed in Canada with $30 to my name, this was a fortune.

What a thrill it was to enter the great stone archway of this impressive 1832 restored fortress, manned primarily by students. I never grew tired of watching one hundred and thirty of Ontario's finest hunks, outfitted in full dress uniform made in England with bearskins, red woollen jackets and polished black boots, as they re-enacted battles each day before scores of tourists. The temperature on the parade square was over 100°F; I don't know how they managed to do their work in the heavy-duty uniforms. My office overlooked the square, and my lasting memory as I pored over the pay chits was the continuous sound of the fife and drum bands interspersed with the firing of cannons.

That June we prepared for a visit by the Queen of England. My boss said that he had a really important job for me that day. Maybe because I was the token Brit, he wanted me to hand over the flowers? But no, my job was to test the pen Her Majesty was going to use to sign the visitors' book to make sure it was working properly. On the day the closest I got to the Queen was to have my photo taken in the chair she sat in.

Every morning I'd don my matching uniform of white blouse, red blazer and navy skirt and swagger down the street, revelling in my good fortune. To tell the truth, I felt more like a volunteer at a holiday camp! And bearing in mind that there were 130 men and only 35 women, there was a lot of fun to be had – an endless round of parties and events I'd never heard of, such as corn boils and wiener roasts.

I seemed to fall in love a lot that summer, but one particular pal was Henry Knotek. His family came from Czechoslovakia and his typical Czech mama took great pride in trying to fatten me up with her goulash and dumplings. Henry, I seem to remember, spent most of his time in the stockyard of the fort, paying for his rebel attitudes, but he went on to become one of the most successful lawyers in Ontario. This whole period was one of the greatest horizon-broadeners, living and working amongst so many nationalities, and it probably set the pattern of attitudes for the rest of my life.

A typist at the fort did some part-time singing on the television. I told her about my own show-business experiences and she invited me to the local station, CKWS, to watch her perform on a programme called 'Lunchbox'. Afterwards she introduced me to the producer and off-handedly mentioned, 'Oh, Gloria here is from Ireland. She sings as well.'

The producer's eyes lit up. 'Do you known any Irish songs?'

I said I did and promptly launched into 'Forty Shades

of Green'. The producer was so impressed that I was instantly on the bill. To tell the truth, with Canada's immigrant population anyone who could sing an Irish song in tune and who had a ready repertoire of Irish favourites was in great demand. From CKWS I moved on to another station where I was given my own weekly request show. The fifteen-minute slot featured my vocals backed by a trio of piano, bass and drums. Listeners would either call or write in their requests, and I was thrilled to oblige. 'Mrs O'Hanlon from Marysville would like to hear "When Irish Eyes Are Smiling", and here it is!' Eventually I went on to perform on many local television variety shows as well. I couldn't help but think back on those days of singing lustily into our Bakelite waiting to be discovered. Now it was all really happening.

The Royal Military College, an all-male domain, was based right below the fort. One day we were surprised to see that the College had advertised for cheerleaders in their magazine, and my room-mate Eleanor and I found ourselves on the team. The College magazine was to write: 'The female has invaded R.M.C. in the peaceful, distracting guise of cheerleaders', but very soon we were on the sidelines yelling our chants – pearls of wisdom like:

> Yell out the cheer
> Reach for a 'C'
> Here come the boys
> From R.M.C.
>
> A boom a lak – a boom a lak
> Boom a lak a bee

Chick a lak – chick a lak
Chick a lak a chee
A boom a lak
Chick a lak
Chick a lak a chee
R.B.C. Whee-ee-ee

What's the matter can't you take it
Can't you Alabamy shake it
Can't you boogie to the right
Can't you boogie to the left
Shouting R.M.C.
Fight – fight – fight

If the chants were a bit banal, the men weren't, because it was on the pitch that I met my first serious love. Walter Moore, a member of the football team, was the most strikingly handsome man I'd ever seen. The cheerleader and the football hero: it was a dreadfully clichéd pairing that I would never quite live down, but I was madly in love.

By today's standards, of course, our courtship was impossibly innocent. We shared candlelit diners, went ice skating, pony-trekking and deep-sea fishing, and attended all the campus activities including an abundance of football banquets and teas. I was introduced to the North American college tradition of being 'pinned', one step short of an engagement ring; but, having been raised on hellfire and brimstone, I still adhered to rigid limits of sexual behaviour. We probably did everything but the deed; however, sex outside marriage was still strictly taboo. Bearing a child out of wedlock was the ultimate disgrace. The only time my mother had ever touched on sex education was to ask, 'Are they teaching you about womanly matters up there at the college?' I answered with a terse and embarrassed yes, and the matter was summarily dropped.

Shortly before Christmas Dad wrote me a very touching letter cautioning me against pre-marital sex. 'I understand you've met this boy and I know how feelings can run high, particularly with the pain of parting. But remember, keep yourself intact. Don't *ever* give in . . .' So I let Walt know what a good Irish girl wouldn't do.

I kept my word to my parents and sailed home for the holidays. I left two thirds of my clothes behind and took just enough money for my return trip. My plan was to spend three months in Portadown and then go back to Canada in April for Walt's graduation. I didn't know how I would bear the time without him. He had asked me to marry him and upon graduation we planned to move out to Vancouver. Of course, my parents were mortified when I told them. In fact, when Mum realised how serious this plan was she wouldn't even discuss it. To her mind it was like losing me forever.

As the weeks wore on I found myself in a quandary. Yes, I was mad for this man and one part of me wanted desperately to marry him. But ours had been a whirlwind courtship of only a few months. Did I really know him well enough? And moving to Vancouver, 3,500 miles from Kingston, would place me a staggering 6,500 miles away from home, literally halfway around the world.

As April drew near my parents were determined I should stay right where I was. After all, I was only eighteen. Dad approached me one morning with a job advertisement. 'There's a position for a production assistant in Ulster Television. Sounds very exciting. I think maybe you should apply.'

5

Getting Hitched

I recognised instantly that here was a singularly rare opportunity. Ulster Television was the first independent network in Northern Ireland. Imagine being part of history, of working at this exciting new media frontier. I believe there are certain people and events that are sent to you at crucial turning points in your life. I reasoned that if I won the job then I was meant to remain in Ireland. If it didn't come through, however, then I'd carry out my initial plan and return to Canada.

Determined to make a bold impression, I breezed into the interview dressed in a white leather fur-lined hooded coat with matching boots. Underneath was a spectacular black dress I'd bought in Ontario. Here I was, Gloria Hunniford, world traveller, just back from abroad with a hint of a Canadian accent. I'd done radio and television, had a big celebrity write-up in the local paper: teenage star and all that.

As it turned out, I didn't get the job as production assistant, though they did offer me a position in the sales department. Fate, it seemed, had settled my wager. I'd go back to Kingston as planned. Meantime, this job certainly was a step up from the chicken factory where I was currently employed selling Rhode Island Reds, so I accepted the offer as a temporary measure.

My boss, Basil Lapworth, began calling me 'Hunni', a nickname I'd never been given before. The moniker stuck and whenever I go back to UTV that's all I get. I was to spend most of my day typing, filing and helping run the office.

On the very first day the managing director, Brum Henderson, was minus a secretary. So I was summoned to the boardroom to take a letter. I was petrified yet aware of the opportunity to make an instant impression. I sat down quietly, pen in hand, confident in my shorthand skills. The first word to come out of Mr Henderson's mouth was 'Felicitations'. As his dictation progressed it became clear that here was the most verbose man in the whole of Ireland. His command of the English language was superb, but he never used one simple word when ten complicated ones would do. My heart pounded as I scrambled to piece together the words phonetically. This agony went on for pages until I filled an entire notebook. Of course, I was too nervous and embarrassed to ask what the hell these words meant.

I was staying temporarily with Lena, who lived just ten miles from Belfast. That night we pored over my notes, tossing out whole paragraphs, cutting the material to a mere third of the original. I typed it up and the next morning handed it to Mr Henderson. He never said a word to me, apparently never even noticing. As time went on I would tell him, 'I'm the best subeditor you've ever had.' He, in turn, would give me advice like 'Never marry for money, but do your courting where there's a bit of it around.' He told me something else too: that I would definitely go on to better things.

The tea-time news programme at Ulster Television had begun to attract a slate of major names from the British entertainment industry: Joe Loss and his orchestra, Emile Ford and the Checkmates, Acker Bilk and his band. Also coming over to the theatre were people like Richard Todd and Beatrice Lillie. Starstruck as ever, I saw an opportunity to mingle with the big names. I knew that the bosses regularly entertained the guests in the boardroom after the programme. One day I boldly approached them and offered my services. 'Would you like me to pour drinks for the guests? I'm not doing anything tonight. I wouldn't mind at all.'

Here I was, young, seven stone one, ambitious and enthusiastic. I soon made myself indispensable in the boardroom, chatting up the luminaries, making sure I always had my photo snapped with them by the studio photographer. Every weekend when I went home I'd produce the shots and tell my parents, 'Guess who I met this week?'

Only six weeks into the job I was approached about another opening for a production assistant. 'Had there been two appointments at the time you would have got it,' I was told. 'Are you still interested?' Of course I was, but this was crunch time. After much agonising I wrote to Walt and broke the news that I wasn't coming back. I've often wondered what might have been had I decided to return to Canada and marry. Would I be a housewife living in Vancouver somewhere? Such is life. After a letter of disbelief and disappointment, I never heard from him again.

I was now in the world of 'darling' and 'luvvie'. 'Darling, would you do this?' 'Luvvie, would you bring that scriptboard here?' As a production assistant I was responsible for timing the programmes, and collating information, captions and camera directions. It was the early nerve-racking days of live television, a pressured, often frenetic job, as there was only one PA on duty at any given time. We ran an hour-long women's show at 4:30 called 'A Matter of Taste'. At half past five I'd gather up all my captions, theme music, timing notes and contracts and race upstairs to my office, dumping it all and lifting the next bundle for the news programme at 6:00.

You had to be on top of it. I was calling the shots, backtiming the programme, which meant I had to know all the camera line-ups and crossovers. Of course, it was all splendid training for the future. To this day the one thing I can do as a broadcaster is read a clock.

Our commercial breaks back then were not always of the thirty-to-sixty second variety seen today, but were often lengthy dramatic productions known as Advertising Magazines. A ten- or thirteen-minute storyline was written around the sponsor's products and acted out just like a drama sketch. 'Good morning, John, would you pass me those delicious Kellogg's cornflakes?' 'Why sure, Donna. And I'm certain you'll want some Tate and Lyle sugar on those. Say, Donna, did you happen to notice this terrific Robinson and Cleaver jacket I'm wearing to work today?' I don't know how the actors ever managed to keep a straight face.

All together, there were around seventy of us employed at UTV, a brilliant assemblage of young talent, with many becoming famous names, including Anne Gregg, who went on to do the BBC holiday programme, and Ivor Mills, who became a national newsreader for ITN. One of the floor managers was Derek Bailey, the now prestigious arts director and producer, who started the same day as I did. He told me that he and his wife had sent out letters every single week for two years trying to land a job in television. I was impressed by that kind of persistence, especially when things had come so easy for me thus far. It was a lesson I later passed on to my children when the time came for their own search for work. Keep knocking on doors.

I'll always remember Derek, too, for putting me in my place. He was directing the sports coverage one evening when I was on duty. On my break I went to a local pub, Studio 3, or Dirty Dick's, as we called it, where somebody suggested I should have a Tia Maria, which I thought was very upmarket. Stupidly I went on drinking them. By the time the programme began my head was reeling. Forget trying to time the show, the numbers on my stopwatch were a complete blur. The director had to carry me that day as I could barely stand, and soon I was wildly sick. Later Derek took me aside. 'In this business even one slip-up could mean disaster. People are depending on you. Don't ever drink before a show again.' It was a mistake I have never repeated. With live broadcasting, there's enough to go wrong without alcohol.

Our two directors at the network were Michael Kent, a dear friend who today lives in London, and John Scholtz-Conway, the director I worked with most of the time. John called all of us darling, including his wife Terri. Quite often she would sit in the control box while he was working and if he said, 'Darling, can I have a cup of tea?' the two of us would jump to his attention. John discovered Roger Whitaker. When no one showed any interest in Roger in England John brought him over to Northern Ireland and produced a series with him on which I was the PA. Programmers in the regions snapped him up and he went on to become the international star he is today. I've since interviewed Roger many times over the years and am proud to say he still uses my scriptboard which he pinched from me over thirty years ago.

I also worked with comedian Frank Carson who got his first big break on UTV. He hosted a variety programme whimsically titled 'Come On On On On In'. From a homely Irish kitchen Frank would introduce as many as fifteen quests per week, singers, dancers and novelty acts. The entire artists' fee was contained in an incredible shoestring budget of just one hundred pounds – I remember because I typed the contract.

My parents wanted me to travel to UTV in Belfast from Portadown daily on the train, but with this totally new and exciting social life opening up the idea was completely impractical. So a friend of mine from Portadown, Suzy Gibson, and another pal, Liz McFetrich, decided to share a flat. It was in the university area of Belfast, which I thought was very posh. It boasted a large living room complete with a piano for the many parties we hosted. The bedroom, though, was another story altogether: three beds and no floor space. As soon as I opened the bedroom door I had to clamber over nothing but bed to get at my own. There was no heating in the flat, but I remember we wore these terribly unsexy flannelette pyjamas with a warm cardy on top. It was all rollers in the hair, face cream and nylons in the shower. Never a stitch of privacy, but who cared? We were bachelor girls on the loose in Belfast having a grand time.

Soon we decided our surroundings could be even

grander, and we moved to a very stately street of houses, Wellington Park. It was still a one-bedroom flat, but this time a huge bedroom to accommodate the three single beds. There was always a party going on, but Tuesday nights we always looked forward to; that was the big night at Maxim's Dancehall in central Belfast. Drinks at the flat before we went consisted of two bottles of Merry down cider at five shillings each and a packet of ciggies. I was a non-smoker, but tried desperately to join in with the rest, because I rather fancied myself with a cigarette-holder. Fortunately it never caught on.

Eventually our rowdy parties got us into trouble. The landlord decided the neighbours couldn't tolerate the music and the comings and goings any longer, so we were turfed out. I was petrified my parents would find out, but was rescued by a friend from Portadown, Felicity Carrier. Flick's grandfather owned Wade's pottery, and her parents ran the Northern Ireland branch. They allowed us to live in their Belfast flat in the elegant area of Lennoxvale Gardens. I found myself surrounded by the most exquisite furniture and artefacts; this, combined with the excitement of a television job, made me feel it was all happening. On reflection, Flick's Mum, Iris, taught me how to appreciate fine wood and china, and I'm convinced she kindled my great love of antiques.

Social life at UTV was bustling. Everyone at the station was young and single and we moved around en masse, spending weekends and holidays together. Apart from a constant round of dinners and parties, we did our fair share of pony trekking and fishing as well. When we went deep-sea fishing off Donaghadee I fell horribly ill within the first half hour. For the rest of the day I had to lie flat on my back with a string attached to my toe. It was the only way I could manage!

I was being exposed to a whole new spectrum of experiences. My mother's cooking, while hearty and delicious, was plain by big city standards. Mum would never have served us anything like curry or spaghetti – 'trash food' she would call it. But now I was dining at Belfast's finer restaurants and acquiring a sophisticated palette. I was forever ordering Nuits St Georges wine. My party was impressed when I tripped out this expensive order to the waiter; little did they realise it was the only wine I knew!

For a short time I dated the dashing and well-to-do wealthy Basil Tittrington. He invited me for a New Year's Eve dinner at his parents' elegant manor home in Dunmurry, just outside Belfast. Once seated in the imposing formal dining room I took in the place settings, each with cutlery five utensils deep. Would I select the wrong fork for the salad? Then Basil's mother placed a silver dish of pâté in front of me. All I could think of was Shipton's Paste; I had no idea what you did with it. 'Oh, not for me, thank you. Actually I don't ever eat it at all,' I said.

'But it's my own,' she insisted, obviously affronted. 'You know, I'm quite famous locally for my pâté.'

'No, honestly, I just couldn't.'

I watched the guests around the table and saw how this delicacy was spread on bits of toast. 'Oh, I've changed my mind,' I told my hostess as nonchalantly as possible. But to save face I added, 'Sometimes it just doesn't agree with me.' I met Basil recently on a plane from London to Belfast, and we had many a laugh over those early days.

Around the halls of Ulster Television there was always a

buzz of speculation whenever a new boy arrived on the scene. Not long after I started a hotshot cameraman named Don Keating turned up. He was immediately nick-named 'poetry in motion' for his fluid, near seamless rhythm with a camera. He'd been brought over from ABC in Didsbury in Manchester to help run the fledgeling network. You could call it hate at first sight. First of all, I thought he was arrogant because he spoke with an English accent. 'He's a bit off-hand, isn't he?' I remarked to my girlfriends. I don't think he liked me much either. The truth was, he completely ignored me and promptly took up with the make-up girl, which, strangely, infuriated me even further.

But because we all ran around together Don and I got to know each other quite well without really trying. His roots, I discovered, were in Youghal in County Cork in the Irish Republic, where he'd lived until the age of eight. He told stories of going out in the rowboats and how scampi were known as the scavengers of the sea, used only for bait until they began to be exported to France and became all the rage. Don's father made a modest fortune in the hotel business, but then when that went sour he moved the family to Manchester and built up a trade in kosher food for the Jewish community.

Don was an accomplished athlete, good at football and cricket. He told me about his early bid to join the Navy. On the morning he was scheduled to sign up, he pulled back the curtain to witness a full force gale blow-ing. 'Blast it, I'm not going to sea today,' he decided and went back to bed. That same day he got a call from ABC Television in Didsbury about becoming a trainee camera-man. Don got into the adventurous world of live television, where at that time nothing was recorded.

He was assigned to live drama known as 'armchair theatre', a staggering task of blocking, timing and detailed shot calling. He often tells the most extraordinary story of one particular programme in 1958: 'We were doing a one-hour drama called *Underground* about the aftermath of a tube explosion. All was proceeding normally until the beginning of the second act when one of the three leads, Gareth Jones, abruptly keeled over. This wasn't in the script so Mike Kent (who was acting as assistant camera-man) rushed over and with the help of a prop man dragged the guy out to the scene dock. We then heard this poor fellow give a death rattle and, incredibly, he expired right there in Mike's arms.

'By this time the third act had begun and the shot was the whole of the studio on a forty-five degree wide-angle lens. In the midst of this opening scene where the actors were supposed to be sleeping, poor Mike was running madly about the set calling for the house doctor. Through my radio cans I heard the director Ted Kotchev in a frenzy, crying out, "There's somebody in shot. There's somebody in shot . . . Get that git outta shot!"

'The entire third act was, of course, total ad lib. The remaining two leads busked the entire drama which was all complicated dialogue. Simply extraordinary. After-wards, we expected a flood of calls. There were only three, however, inquiring about the third actor. The poor sod wasn't even missed!'

After several months of tentative approaches, Don and I finally dropped the silly charade and our true feel-ings spilled out. One date led to another and I had to admit I was falling deeply in love with this good-looking, intense, blue-eyed man. I remember him cooking me dinner in my flat, and my thinking, 'This is the man I should spend the rest of my life with. At least he can make up for my lack of culinary skill – maybe.' A year and a half after we'd just met, when I'd just turned twenty-one, we decided to get married. Standing in our way, however, was one monumental roadblock. He was a Catholic.

In Ireland, even in 1961 this was scandalous, almost like a white marrying a black in the American deep south. We were about to cross forbidden lines which had been drawn for centuries. To many people interreligious pairings were considered as downright traitorous.

I dreaded telling my parents. To complicate matters, they'd never even met Don. I'd been too scared they'd find out about his religion. He wanted to accompany me to break the news, but this was something I knew I could only handle alone.

'Do you realise what you're saying?' my Dad erupted. 'You can't marry a Catholic. I'm a member of the Orange Order. What would the neighbours say?'

'Whatever has that got to do with anything? Look, it's just an accident of birth.'

'I couldn't show my face again at another meeting. I couldn't walk in the Twelfth of July parade. What would the Orangemen think?'

'But I really want you at the wedding – you're my parents. Wait till you meet our UTV priest, Father Hugh Murphy – he's such a wonderful, liberal man.'

'You're asking your mother and me to sit in a Catholic church? And see our daughter married by a Catholic priest? What can you be thinking, girl?'

'But Don's an *English* Catholic. It's nothing like as rigid. . . .'

Finally, Dad laid the law down. 'Gloria, look here. If

you marry this fella, I cannot and will not go to the wedding.'

I looked at Mum but she said, 'I'm sorry, dear. I certainly can't go if your father won't.' Later she confessed that this was the most heartbreaking decision she'd ever made, and that missing my wedding was the single greatest regret of her life.

I burst into tears and ran upstairs, shattered and distraught. After all, what girl doesn't want her parents at her side on the most joyful and blessed day of her life? I thought back to Canada, that society where people were just people, heedless of race or religion. Why couldn't we be happy like that?

But I wouldn't be put off, even by my own family. I loved Don and I was determined to marry him.

Later that evening Dad approached me with a surprising compromise. 'If you go ahead, you know we can't be there on principle. But if you do, everything will be fine afterwards. There won't be any rift. We'll welcome your Don as part of the family.' My father kept his word and once the ceremony was over, Don became his own son in every way. Mum told me later that my wedding day was a nightmare for her. She plotted the timetable in her head, trying to imagine what was happening. She was agonised that, because of Dad's stubbornness, she couldn't be in her rightful place.

In the absence of my parents my Dad's sister, Aunt May, and Uncle Jim Menaul helped me to plan the wedding, select my dress and let me stay at their house the night before the ceremony. And Uncle Jim proudly volunteered to give me away. They were extremely kind to me, and created a loving family atmosphere leading up to the big day.

It was a wedding day as special and memorable as every girl dreams. Lena and her husband provided close family support for which I'll be forever grateful. In a very moving ceremony, Don and I were joined as husband and wife by Father Hugh Murphy.

The reception, held at Belfast's Wellington Park Hotel, was totally devoid of the usual formality of these occasions. There were no long-winded speeches, no elder statesmen to keep us in check, and in the absence of most of our family our one hundred invited guests felt free to let their hair down. Don's best man Mike Kent, thoroughly oiled from a steady stream of 'sherbets', gave only a brief toast. 'I can't understand why people are always so damn happy at weddings,' he babbled. 'All your troubles are just beginning. They should be happy instead at funerals when all their troubles are finished.'

As we set off for our honeymoon in Southern Ireland, we tumbled into a car adorned with the traditional 'Just Married' signs, tethered cans and clouds of confetti. Then on the drive to Dublin Don and I kept noticing an odd odour that soon became intolerable. We finally stopped the car, opened the bonnet and discovered a string of kippers stuck and baking in the engine.

That night we'd no sooner checked into the Gresham Hotel than we got a call from the front desk. Friends of ours were waiting in the lobby, we were told. Don and I figured it must be a mistake. Reluctantly we came downstairs to find Morris, one of the soundmen from the station, and his wife, fresh from the reception. In their inebriated and enthusiastic state they had followed us all the way to Dublin. Not only that, but they insisted on having dinner with us! I couldn't wait to get rid of them.

At last we managed to usher them into their car and

steer them in the general direction of Belfast. I joked to Don that I was finally going to get my wicked way with him. There is definitely something to be said for waiting. In my head I could hear my mother's words, 'All good girls save themselves for the man they're going to marry.' I was glad that I had.

Following the honeymoon Don and I rented a little place on Cedar Avenue in Belfast. Since the policy of the network forbade husband and wife to work in the same department I was forced to quit my job. Settling into my new role as a housewife was no minor adjustment. As a cook, I was a newly wedded husband's worst nightmare. My stew was barely edible, and my custards were like water. In exasperation I would ring Don at work, asking, 'How do you make gravy?' My accomplished cook of a husband would patiently relay step-by-step instructions over the phone. One day I determined to surprise him with a magnificent Cornish pasty. I struggled all afternoon baking the crust to golden flaky perfection. I set it on a tray but while making my grand entrance I tripped, sending my masterpiece splattering to the floor. While Don tried to muffle his laughter, I angrily scooped it up. 'You're going to eat it anyway!' I said. And he did.

I made a further fool of myself one afternoon at the butcher's shop on the corner, by asking for pork chops and bacon. I could feel the customer's eyes regarding me strangely. The butcher told me 'Miss, don't you know this is a Jewish shop? We only sell kosher.' I twirled around and scampered out the door, my face scarlet with embarrassment.

We soon moved to another rented house on Hollywood Road in Belfast. I will always remember the place for two events: the great snows of 1962 and the birth of our first child. With my being pregnant and with the snow waist-high the neighbours helped out. Ernest and Roberta McConville, who lived opposite, did the shopping, shared the food and created a warm depth of friendship that exists to this day.

Don and I were thrilled to be expecting in our very first year of marriage. But if you looked at me you'd never have known I was pregnant. I was sick every hour of every day. I couldn't eat and as a result began losing weight. I didn't even wear maternity clothes until my seventh month. All this coincided with the outbreak of the thalidomide scare. Immediately I heard about it I panicked, terrified that perhaps I'd inadvertently taken some of the dreaded tablets – was that why I was so ill? For the twenty-four hours it took to make contact with my doctor I kept imagining the worst. Miraculously, my doctor confirmed he'd never prescribed the drug for my sickness.

Towards the end of the seventh month Don and I decided a short holiday away from home would do me good, so we travelled to London to visit friends and see a production of *Oliver*. In the middle of Ron Moody's antics as Fagin I experienced a sudden irresistible urge to go to the loo. I just made it when my waters burst. I wasn't due for two months, but I knew this was the signal the baby was coming.

I hurried back to my seat and whispered frantically to Don, 'My waters have broken.' Absorbed in the musical, he said 'Shhhh' and put me off with a preoccupied wave of his hand – he detested being interrupted in the middle of a show.

'My waters have broken!' I persisted. 'The baby's coming.'

'Oh my God!' he cried out loud. 'You mean it's all happening now?' He fell out of his seat, helped me out to the lobby and an ambulance was called. Racing through the heart of London, the siren blaring, we reached Charing Cross Hospital only to be turned away. 'Sorry,' came the word. 'All filed up.' It was like no room at the inn.

I'd never heard of such a thing. Did they want my baby to be born in the back of an ambulance? The contractions were rolling over me in waves. 'If it's a boy,' joked Don, 'we'll have to call him Oliver.' We sped through the unfamiliar London streets, finally pulling up at St Mary's, By now it was past 11:00 and once I was settled in the doctor told Don, 'You may as well come back in the morning. First babies take hours.' Remember, this was still the era when husbands were definitely not encouraged in the delivery room.

Don kissed me goodbye and had no sooner left than in one swift motion out popped the baby eager to get into this world. Though tiny and premature she was otherwise perfect in every way, with an exquisite rosebud mouth. I decided to name her Caron after my screen favourite, Leslie Caron, Gigi herself. Don adored her on sight. We were now a real family. Afterwards, I was on such a high from the pethodine painkiller that I was gabbling away to the doctor and nurses, exclaiming this was my first tea party at three o'clock in the morning. Twenty-eight years later, on Caron's wedding day, one of the wonderful surprises was a telegram from Lionel Bart, the composer of *Oliver*, saying she must come back and see the show properly some time.

Right after Caron's birth I weighed six stone ten

pounds, like something out of Belsen. And we weren't going to get away from sickness, because Caron guzzled my milk so fast she had projectile vomiting, which meant I seemed to spend all my time in one corner of the room with towels spread out over the floor in the opposite corner. It was a real hit-or-miss affair. One day when I was breastfeeding her a friend's little boy said, 'What are you doing?' I said, 'I'm giving the baby her milk.' 'Oh,' he replied. 'Does she get her dinner out of the other one?'

It was ironic that my parents weren't at the wedding, and, due to circumstances, couldn't be around for the birth of Caron. But in a strange way it was a rather special time, because it was the three of us against the world. My sister Lena by this stage had two lovely sons, Laurence and Nigel, who was just three months older than Caron, but Caron was the first granddaughter and so was idolised by my parents. When I arrived back in Ireland with quite a souvenir from my visit to London, all the pain of the previous years and the resentment regarding religion disappeared, and the fact that Caron was baptised into the Church of Ireland with my parents and Lena acting as godparents healed any minor crack.

I think it is only when you have a child of your own that you fully appreciate your parents. I remember writing to them from the hospital, saying, 'If Don and I can be anything like you as parents, then we'll be very complete.' I was to find this letter amongst my mother's things after she died.

Now that there were three of us Don and I decided to save for a home of our own, although things were a bit tight. Rows would erupt over the silliest matters. Once I spent five shillings on a waste basket, which upset Don no end. 'We didn't need that!' he carped. 'Five shillings for a bloody bin!' Men!

I hated not having money of my own. I wasn't used to it. I'd been making money all my life. I determined that never again would I have to justify buying a pair of shoes to Don or anyone else. So immediately I went out and got myself a job with Avon cosmetics, which was totally new in Northern Ireland, and quite a novelty. I became Gloria Hunniford, the local 'ding-dong' lady. After settling Caron in the pram I'd pack the cosmetics beneath the cover and push her around the neighbourhood making deliveries. I made just about enough for pin money.

Our search for a house took us ten miles from Belfast, to a show house in Marnabrae Park in Lisburn, where a builder was constructing American-style bungalows. You walked into a small hallway that opened up into one central living area. Step down into the sunken lounge, step up into the dining area. It was so spacious and airy, complete with central heating, totally different from anything I was used to. I leaned up against the spectacular stone fireplace and sighed, 'Now this is style!' I thought I was on millionaires' row.

The price was £2,800 and £300 extra for heating. On a thirty-year mortgage it worked out to a little over twenty-nine pounds a month. Just within our budget.

We watched it being built, making our own plans to finish it off. The look at the time was a rough hessian finish on the walls. It was terribly expensive, but we managed to buy a bale of it cheap from a sacking company and it took six of us to handle this huge sticky mass of material. I used to work for hours rubbing the floors with button polish to give the effect of oak floorboards. Mum came over to help make curtains. When she walked through the front door she paused at the natural brick wall. 'Lovely, darling,' she commented. 'Once you get this wall plastered it'll look wonderful.'

The day we moved in the only furniture we had was a cot for Caron, a bed we had bought for a mere ten quid (which Don still has) and two chairs borrowed from my sister. A few cheap mats were scattered on the floor. I remember, months later, the thrill of simply getting some underlay down, never mind actual carpeting. 'Listen Don, we can't hear our feet any more!' I rejoiced. I would have bigger and grander homes, but nothing quite so special as that petite family bungalow.

It was in that neighbourhood that we met Anne Thompson and her husband Billy, soon to the the youngest gynae and obstetrics professor ever in Northern Ireland. Anne remains one of my very best friends to this day. We both had daughters of exactly the same age and both became pregnant with our second children at the same time. Anne and I often look back on those days as the most carefree of our lives. We would walk the two miles to the clinic each week to pick up the babies' milk and buy fish and chips on the way back. Not wanting to be seen eating in the street, we hid the food beneath the pram cover and occasionally stuck our fingers in, inconspicuously stealing a bit here and there all the way home, giggling as we went. We spent nearly every afternoon together – her house one day and mine the next.

Just nine months after delivering Caron, I found myself pregnant again. Towards the end of my term grandmother Hunniford died, upsetting me not merely because of the loss, but because in my condition I couldn't attend her funeral. Don was reluctant to go himself with the baby imminently due. 'I'm not going unless you're admitted to hospital,' he finally ordered. I capitulated and he dropped me off. He settled me in my ward, and as he was leaving he looked back and said, 'Remember Frank

Sinatra – just take it nice and easy.' I wished I had something to throw at him. Almost immediately I felt the contractions begin, and recalled my mother's adage that 'births and deaths often come together'. It was coincidentally her own birthday the next day, 10 June. Just like Caron in the rush to enter the world, Paul came quickly and easily, and like his big sister he was perfect in every way.

Don returned from the funeral just in time to learn the news. He rushed to the nursery and asked the sister to hold up his son to the glass. As she picked up baby Paul, Don caught the shock of bright ginger hair and shook his head. 'No. The name is Keating.'

The nurse nodded, pointing to the infant. 'No. *Keating*,' he insisted. It just didn't sink in that this boy with bright ginger hair could possibly belong to him.

We were blissfully happy, parents of a lovely girl and boy, the proverbial pigeon pair. But now as I entered my middle twenties life was about to take another wide turn. My voice, which I'd come to regard as a reliable, cherished springboard to opportunity, was about to spin me in a direction that would change the course of the rest of my life.

6

It's a Man's World

I resumed my career back on Ulster Television, working the same shows I'd done as a PA, but this time in front of the camera. All those years of pushing that stopwatch at least taught me what was expected in front of camera. I soon became a regular on 'Tea Time With Tommy', a popular musical request programme. Just as in Canada, the audience would write in their favourites and I'd launch into 'Strangers in the Night' or another hit of the day. The host was pianist Tommy James, well known for his party trick of tickling the ivories with two oranges. It sounds outlandishly tame in this day and age, but I promise you it was highly popular.

As the local reputation grew, I also began to branch out. I sang on Radio Telefis Eireann, the official station in Dublin. That I hailed from the North, I think, gave me an extra edge.

1964 saw the beginning of the cabaret scene in Northern Ireland. No dank, smoky basement cellars these, but rather affluent, cosmopolitan nightclubs with names like the Abercorn, Tito's and the Talk of the Town – where, incidentally, Roy Walker, now famous as a comedian, was the resident singer. The most fun to play was the Half Door Club in Bangor, attached to the Royal Hotel. For me it was a round trip of fifty miles, which I did three times a week for the princely fee of four pounds per night. Gone were the days of being accompanied only by a pianist. Now I enjoyed the distinction of being backed by a quartet, quintet or even sextet of accomplished musicians, requiring rigorous rehearsals, usually headed by Marie Murphy – a neighbour and one-time pianist to Ruby Murray.

Not only were the shows more upscale, so was my wardrobe. No simple outfits bought off the rack at the local dress shop would do. The cabaret audience expected glamour and chic. And I knew just where to go – back to my Auntie Myrtle in Portadown. I'll never forget taking the stage at the Abercorn in a silver laminated mini-dress that looked like a belt, set off by a smashing pair of white go-go boots. In later years I was to tease Danny La Rue that I copied a few of his ideas from the telly. I saw him once wearing this absolutely stunning cloak trimmed with feather boas. Since I couldn't afford a proper boa, I merely substituted a double frilling of the material from my dress. When I interviewed Danny years later and mentioned this, he had hysterics.

All this time Don did his share of babysitting while I trundled round the roads at night. My cabaret experience had been going on smoothly for about five years when in 1969 the political troubles in Ireland worsened and things began to fall apart. Driving home at night I'd often run right into a street riot. Finding myself smack in the middle of a harrowing fight I'd have to turn the car around and hastily find an alternative route home. I remember one night in particular on the Hollywood Road in Belfast. I became totally panicked that I couldn't turn the car around and get out in time; all the while cars were being overturned and set on fire, and bricks and bottles were being hurled from side to side. It wasn't unknown to be booked into a club only to get there and find it had been blown up the night before. Looking back, it was a particularly dangerous time for a woman to be travelling the roads alone at night.

One night, having stopped off to see Mum in Portadown after a show, I was driving back home along the motorway. It was wintry and foggy, and my car conked out abruptly. I tried to flag down a passing motorist, but nobody would stop – these *were* dangerous times. The police finally approached and circled around me three times. It turned out they suspected I was a terrorist decoy. Ultimately I was driven home in a police car to a very worried Don.

At this point, my shows on Ulster Television with my old pal Tommy James were called 'In Town with Tommy', and had become much more elaborate, complete with full-blown production numbers. Entertainment producer Rob Harding came over from London to produce these segments, teaching me some choreography and dressing me in even grander style. During one of my appearances I was joined by comedian and songwriter Alan Hawkshawe, and after the show he approached me with a unique opportunity. That year Lulu was Britain's entry in the Eurovision Song Contest, and had performed one of Alan's songs on the television programme which made the ultimate choice. Sadly, his song hadn't made it, but nevertheless he thought it would be ideal for me: 'Why don't you record it, and we'll release it as a single in Ireland?' The song was 'Are You Ready for Love?' The backing track was already arranged. Now this was big time!

Just like that, a trip to London was arranged and I found myself in a proper recording studio. As I walked in the door who should pass me but Sacha Distel, the Paris-born Grammy-winning jazz and pop star. Wow! Entering a tiny cubicle, I could barely contain my excitement upon hearing the playback of my voice over the exact same backing track used by Lulu. To round off one of the most satisfying, perfect days of my life, my old pal Mike Kent (now living in England) took me out for a spectacular dinner at the elegant Carlton Tower Hotel to celebrate, and then put me back on the plane to Belfast late at night, a very happy girl.

Soon I was into the world of plugging my record. Just to think that my song would come out of that old Bakelite wireless set! I got a lot of radio play all over Ireland, and, much to my astonishment, 'Are You Ready for Love?' on the Tangerine label reached a whopping number eight in the Ulster charts. Overnight it was 'Local Lisburn Housewife Top of the Charts'. I was booked for television appearances on all three networks. Still, nothing prepared me for the call from 'Good Morning Ulster', Northern Ireland's equivalent of London's 'Today' programme. In the interview the questions came thick and fast. 'How does it feel to be an overnight sensation? How are you coping with your sudden notoriety? How do you balance career, home and family?' I found it overwhelming, but also terribly thrilling.

Still, I had no idea of the far-reaching impact of that one little record until the phone rang the morning after the interview. The programme's producer, Dan Gilbert, said, 'I was very impressed with the way you handled yourself yesterday – not short of a word or two! Have you ever thought of becoming an interviewer?'

I brushed this suggestion aside. I was a cabaret singer now, a recording artist poised on the edge of something big. 'Mr Gilbert, I'm very flattered but I really don't think. . . .'

'Listen, I'm desperate for a female interviewer. I'm losing two of my best people. One, Diane Harron, is going on to the newsroom; the other, Pat Lindsey, has left to become a producer. What I need is someone to do the voice pieces and some interviewing.'

I had to hand it to him. To have any woman at all in the newsroom was virtually unheard of. At that time you could count on one hand the number of female interviewers in the broadcasting arena. In a male-dominated age this gentleman was far, far ahead of his time. But, as I say, I was a singer. That's all I ever aspired to be, ever dreamed of, and now it was all really happening. . . .

'How about coming in for an interview?' he pressed. 'What have you got to lose?'

Looking back, when I think of the competition today I can't believe how incredibly blasé I was. After all, he had asked me – I hadn't applied for any job. My mother and I had planned a day of shopping in Belfast, and smugly I promised to try to fit him in somehow. I pulled up outside Broadcasting House in my green Mini estate car and told Mum, 'I won't be long. I'm just nipping in to see this producer. He's asked me to be an interviewer. Can you believe it?'

I made my way up to Dan Gilbert's office and we chatted pleasantly for a bit. Again he praised my BBC appearance and asked, 'Wouldn't you just consider the position?'

'Well, I might,' I replied, perhaps a bit too coyly.

'Look, I've got a tape recorder here,' he said, pulling out the machine. 'I'd like you to do a test interview.'

What's this? I thought. What a cheek, this Gilbert. I mean, he asked me here, but he never said anything about an audition . . . .

I wasn't prepared or psyched up for anything like this. Before I could open my mouth to protest, Dan ushered in a woman I recognised as Cicely Matthews of 'Children's Hour'. Now here was a bizarre case of *déjà vu*. 'Children's Hour', the longest running BBC programme ever, had been the first job in broadcasting I'd auditioned for, as a singer – for this very same Cicely Matthews. I failed, though, because the format called for prowess in semi-classical pieces, while I was only interested in the popular hits of the day. Now this woman was retiring from the BBC and I was interviewing her. Whether it was a case of my fury over Gilbert springing this on me or of not being adequately prepared, I felt the subsequent conversation floundered badly. I was certain it answered any question about my future in the broadcast field.

'That's the end of that little episode,' I told my mother as we drove away. 'How dare he give me an interview on the spot? I didn't even ask for a bloody job. I'll never hear from him again, I'm sure.' Even as I said it, I wondered why I was letting it bother me so. After all, I didn't even want it, right?

I'd barely stepped into the house that night when the phone rang. It was Dan Gilbert. 'Terrific, Hunniford. When can you start?'

In a split-second moment of decision the astonishing

words spilled out of my mouth. 'How about tomorrow?' It was only later I was able to reason it out. The truth was, as much as I loved singing, I'd grown weary of the dangerous long night drives.

My new-found broadcasting career didn't exactly burn up the airways. It was a part-time occupation consisting of doing ad hoc interviews on a freelance basis. I had to come up with my own story ideas, which was something I felt I had a nose for; throughout my daily travels, whether shopping, at the hairdresser or at parties, I always kept my ear to the ground for what the public was talking about, things they were genuinely interested in. Next I had to convince my producer to give me the green light. There were several reporters, all of us competing for precious air time. We were all hungry, which brought out the best in us and made for an exciting show. The ultimate goal was to get on air all five mornings, but if you managed two or three you were doing well. We were only paid per story and then just a few pounds each.

Don was by now a director, and used to handling interviews, and was very supportive of my budding new career. He took the time to run through all the newspapers, circling possible story ideas. I remember one day I came back from an interview several hours long. He took one look at my pile of notes and said, 'How are you going to whittle all that down to just three minutes?' For all my enthusiasm it was clear I still had a lot to learn.

One of the best lessons in my broadcasting career came from Dan Gilbert. He said, 'Don't ever think you're here to do fashion, cooking and light stuff, because as far as I'm concerned everyone here is equal and everyone does the same work. You're as good as any man here when it comes to broadcasting. You'll be out there on the streets covering current events just like the fellas. Do I make myself clear?'

Once again, Dan set the tone for equality in the newsroom. Ever since that moment I've never thought myself less able in broadcasting terms than any man.

I'd only been on the job three months when I discovered I was pregnant for the third time. It was bittersweet news. I felt certain I was not destined, after all, for a career in broadcasting. Surely the top brass were never going to allow a woman reporter on the job with an infant in tow? Cautiously I approached Dan and told him the news. To my complete surprise he looked me straight in the eye and said, 'Listen, as long as you can fit behind that microphone , you'll be there, even if we have to cut a lump out of the bloody table!' This wonderful man once again proved himself liberated long before such issues had found their way into public debate.

Just as Dan ordered, I worked right up to the day the baby was born. As my due date came close to Christmas I decided to have labour induced so I could be home for the holidays. Ordinarily I wouldn't have considered that option, but I knew I'd be in good hands. Dr Billy Thompson, husband of my best friend Anne, and by now an eminent gynaecologist, agreed to deliver my baby at the Royal Victoria Hospital, Belfast.

The day before I was due to go into hospital I got into the lift at Broadcasting House and chatted pleasantly with our controller of programmes as we rode down. 'When's the baby due?' he asked.

'Tomorrow,' I answered casually. His whole face suddenly contorted. You never saw anyone so anxious to get out of a lift in your life!

I entered the hospital a week before Christmas, fully anticipating a birth as easy and quick as my first two. I had no sooner been induced, however, than I realised it may have been a very bad idea. The little fella wasn't yet ready to make his appearance. The slow hours of totally wrenching pain that followed were new to me. It seemed days before I was wheeled into the delivery room to the comforting sight of Billy, and then at last all was forgotten in the joy of having my son delivered into the world by my cherished friend. Michael was born at 5:30 pm on 16 December, 1970. Billy and Anne were godparents. Coming home for Christmas was a delight. After all, we'd had the best gift. Caron, however, had flu and was totally uninterested. But all my fears subsided alongside Caron's temperature, and very soon she became a little mother to Michael. To this day they are very close. Recently we've been teasing Michael, as he starts his own broadcasting career, that all that sitting at the microphone in the womb has its advantages.

Two weeks later I returned to my job, working doubly, triply hard to make certain no one would ever point the finger and say I was neglecting the children in any way. Ireland was still very much a chauvinist stronghold, where professional working women, especially those with small children, were not the norm. The burden of proof now rested squarely on my shoulders.

Fortunately, my freelance working hours dovetailed nicely with the demands of family life. I'd get the kids off to school in the morning and maybe call on my pal Anne to babysit. When conflicts arose, I simply bundled

Michael up and took him with me to the studio. BBC Northern Ireland was far ahead of its time in that regard. No one ever gave me the slightest hassle. It was such a warm, friendly, family atmosphere, from which companies today could well take a lesson.

Don, as always, was an enlightened husband and father. We tried to share everything. Amenable to my hectic schedule and my anxiety to make a success of it he willingly started dinner on days I couldn't make it home on time. We tried to share the school runs, but there were times when the schedule went awry; Paul never lets me forget the time he stood waiting at school until 6:00 for me to pick him up – a bad oversight of arrangements on my part. Sometimes I had to stop by the studio on the way home to edit a tape, the kids being content to play cricket or 'Dr Who' in the corridors. Caron fondly remembers eating fish and chips in the canteen for the remarkable cost of five pence. At times it was hard to be everything to everybody, but I tried to make a point of never missing speech days, football games or school concerts.

Still, there was definitely an upside to Mum's unusual profession. Many times when I went out on a story I would take the kids with me. How many kids witness the birth of a baby bear at the zoo or get to look at an ancient ship being dredged up from the depths of the sea? And if my assignment took me to the latest pop concert and I happened to be given a few extra tickets, suddenly Mum was the most popular, terrific, hip mother in the entire world. All of that helped to keep the communication line open.

As freelancers, most of the time we were finding our stories and ideas, and then fixing and researching them ourselves, So, during those rare times when I simply could not get away from home, I engaged in the highly irregular practice of doing in-house interviews. In hindsight I admit it was probably rather bold of me, but nonetheless I'd ring up the person and say, 'Look, if you're coming down my way anyway, why don't you call into my house to do the interview en route?' In order to find a quiet spot I'd invariably lead the subject into my bedroom and close the door behind us. Just recently I had a guest who recalled, 'Remember that interview I did on your bed?' I can only imagine what the tabloids would do with that today!

My reporting skills blossomed under Dan Gilbert's expert tutelage. He was quite simply one of the finest teachers I ever met. For instance, when I started interviewing I used to write out my questions in advance. 'Scrap them!' Dan admonished. 'If you get an unexpected answer, they'll be useless. Talk to the person first, get to know them a little and make notes on interesting points to pick up on.' He also advised: 'Never take your eyes off your subject or try to hide a bungle. It'll almost certainly trip you up and all trust between you and your interviewee will be seriously compromised. And, most important of all, learn to listen.'

With the escalation of the troubles the demands of street reporting became fiercer. I'd be cooking dinner and suddenly get an urgent call. 'There's been an explosion in downtown Belfast. Get down there and cover it.' Naturally I'd have to drop everything and leave at a moment's notice. The worst disaster I ever had to report was the Abercorn bombing. It had been a relatively small explosive, about two pounds, nothing really compared to the five hundred pound bombs that became more commonplace. But it had been planted under a seat in a very crowded restaurant in Belfast's Corn Market on a busy Saturday afternoon, which made for a particularly devastating tragedy.

I arrived on the scene to find sirens blaring all around while police and medical staff desperately tried to establish order amidst throngs of dazed onlookers. Scores of people were littered over the floor, screaming in pain, terror and confusion. Many were badly burned over their entire bodies. Tables were overturned; debris from walls and windows was scattered everywhere. I shuddered at the announcement that two young girls had been killed. The worst twist of fate in this explosion was that one of the two young girls killed turned out to be the daughter of the specialist who'd been called in to perform emergency surgery.

These were not easy stories to cover. One television reporter became so visibly shaken that he broke down on camera, unable to continue. He tried to cover by saying he was out of breath from running up the stairs, but it was clear he was emotionally shattered.

The terrible impact didn't really hit me until the following day. London's 'Today' programme asked for a local reporter to file a story on the lost property office set up to return people's belongings. The assignment was given to me. I remember walking slowly into the grim hallway where the ravaged belongings were all spread out. It was the most heart-wrenching scene I'd ever encountered. There was one shoe, a pair of tights with one leg blown off, a child's charred teddy bear. The force of the bomb had totally flattened good leather handbags. But it was seeing the driver's licence of one of the girls who'd been killed – singed edges around the photo of a bright young face who had everything to live for – that brought home to me how tenuous the thread of life was that we all clung to in those insane, turbulent times. Ordinary, innocent, everyday people of every denomination enjoying a Saturday afternoon of shopping, stopping in for a sandwich or a cup of coffee. All over in one searing second. It was a long while before I could compose myself and continue. I don't believe I've ever completely got over those images and the indescribable futility of it all.

People often ask if I've ever been personally close to a bombing. The answer, unfortunately, is yes. I was about to go on air once in the mid-seventies with a programme called 'What's West' when we were told that a car bomb had been placed at the base of the studio wall and was set to go off in minutes. The building had already been cleared except for a small group of us involved in getting the show on the air. We were given the option to stay or leave. We chose to carry on, rationalising that Broadcasting House was made of stone from top to bottom and as solid as a rock.

This rationalisation did little, however, to calm my nerves. I settled into my seat, nervously clutching my script. Just before we went on air the head of programming, Ronnie Mason, came around with a bottle of brandy. Of course, I'd long ago sworn off ever drinking before a show, but if ever I needed a few swallows this was it. As the programme progressed, minutes seemed like hours, everything running in slow motion.

Suddenly the blast erupted. Under the force of the explosion the entire building rocked and shuddered. I could feel the floor shaking under me like a monster earthquake. Dust came pouring out of the walls and we were told that windows had been blown out over the entire studio block. Mellowed out from the brandy, and my face getting rosier by the second, I'm certain that free-flow broadcast was the best show I ever did. One of the lasting images I have of that day is of my producer rushing outside to plough through the rubble to rescue valuable tapes that had been blasted out on to the street.

Curiously, though, moving out of Northern Ireland was something Don and I never even considered. After all, living in Lisburn, we weren't in one of the danger zones and the children rarely encountered any terrorism first-hand. Yet at the same time it was so ingrained in our psyche that for example on a holiday to Scotland, when we took the kids to see Sweetheart Abbey, a twelfth-century ruin near Dumfries, Paul (then about six) looked up and asked in all innocence, 'Who blew it up?'

The truth is we all had to learn to live with it. Take a hotel like the Europa in central Belfast. It had been blown up over thirty-odd times and whenever I went out to report on it, it was always business as usual, with people clearing up broken glass, nailing up the hardboard, mopping up and starting all over again. The Irish are a resilient lot with a sense of humour that sees them through.

In 1969 I began a ten-year stint working for BFBS, British Forces Broadcasting Service. The purpose of the weekly programme called 'Ulster Calling' was to keep families in touch with their loved ones on the front lines. Servicemen based in BAOR (British Army on the Rhine) would have to leave their families for a four-month tour of duty into Northern Ireland at the very height of the violence. The set-up had me going into the camps to interview the lads, providing a little two-way talk with their loved ones back home. My partner, Sean Rafferty, and I would report any shootings or explosions, allaying fears and sometimes grimly confirming the tragedies on a most personal level, but the main idea was to let the families in Germany know what life on a base camp was like.

I held an officially sanctioned letter from the top military brass allowing me to go into any army base in Ulster. On an early trip to a camp not far from my home, on an old airfield, I encountered first-hand barbed wire fences and lookout posts eerily resembling a Nazi concentration camp. When I questioned the soldiers they said, 'Can't tell you. Top security.' I later discovered this was the construction-in-progress of Long Kesh Prison, so infamous for its conditions it was later renamed the Maze.

On another of my scheduled trips, to a camp in Londonderry, Caron was off school, so I decided to take her with me. We had to leave our car on the outskirts of town and were escorted the rest of the way in a Land Rover. En route we were caught in a heavy crossfire of bullets and bricks. Caron and I hit the floor, huddled close, absolutely petrified. It was the last time I ever took any of my children along for the ride.

Perhaps the most pleasurable occasion during that terrible time was the day I got to drive an army tank. Mine was the lead vehicle poised at the tip of a crisp V-formation. Talk about power! What I wouldn't have given to pull up outside Broadcast House in that baby! Contrary to popular myth, I did not operate the tank in stiletto heels.

Half of Belfast in those trying days was turned into armed military camps, utilising abandoned large houses, factories, old buildings and the like. Often these places were miserable old warehouses with no heat, electricity or even proper plumbing, with three hundred steps to climb up and down endlessly every day. One unusual venue for an army base was The Grand Central Hotel, which I'm sure was the only army base with bathrooms en suite. The top brass received countless invitations to dinners in the private homes of upper-class citizens. The soldiers on the other hand got well used to the 'tea stops' in safe areas, when local citizens would hand out mugs of steaming tea for the boys on patrol. The forces had to cope under very primitive conditions.

I did a lot of interviewing at army messes. One memorable chat was with a soldier whose leg was encased in plaster from ankle to hip. I worried about approaching him, wondering how to bring up his injury. Was it shrapnel from a barrage of bullets or perhaps the savage aftermath of a bomb blast? Finally, I gathered enough courage to come out with it. 'What happened to your leg?'

'It was terrible,' he replied, his eyes suddenly ringed with tears. 'I was at a disco the other night and fell off my platform heels.'

I exploded with laughter. Here was a war story I could really relate to.

Coming from a non-service family I had no idea what a rear party and such army terms meant, so the powers that be decided that a trip to Germany to visit the families back on base would be beneficial. On my first trip while travelling in a military plane, I was sitting up front with the big boys – colonels and generals. To ensure a sterling impression I dressed in a full-length black cossack coat and fox fur hat, the pinnacle of high fashion under siege. As I sat there chatting up the commanding officer, the plane suddenly dipped and my stomach began reeling. As the flight got rougher a hot flush swept my entire body and I became so dizzy I couldn't even talk! I prayed for the strength to make it through the journey. In the presence of such distinguished, dignified military gents, off came the hat and I ripped open my coat, by now a sweaty heap.

At the time we landed I looked at myself, perspiration dripping everywhere, my face a hideous shade of olive green. It certainly cracked the myth of the broadcasting glamour queen. Those trips to Germany showed me the other side of the coin. Commanding officers' wives were left in charge of the morale of the families in camp. What struck me were the teenage girls away from home in a strange country, not knowing what was happening to their husbands in Northern Ireland, and often coping with young children – a trying time for everybody.

After a few years they came to the conclusion that it was too dangerous for us to move about the camps in Northern Ireland, so a decision was made to escort the soldiers into the studio. It was difficult to send really personal messages over the radio. It was usually: 'I'm fine. Hope you and the kids are OK.' 'Miss you, love. Looking forward to coming home soon.' One lad was bold enough to promise, 'I'll be coming in with my boots on.' But the moment that really stands out is one frisky private bellowing into the microphone to his sweetheart. 'Well, luv, it's not long now, but it will be when I get home!' Sean, my co-presenter, and I howled with laughter so much we simply couldn't introduce the next record – this lusty young soldier had to do it for us.

In 1974, when 'Good Morning, Ulster' went off the air for the summer BBC Northern Ireland decided to experiment with a change in format. Instead of the traditional hard news/current affairs slant, a more informal slate of guests, records and chat was introduced. The producers approached me and another journalist, Helen Madden, to present a new show, 'A Week About'. Up until this time Northern Ireland radio had been well scripted. Free-flow, personality-orientated broadcasting had never been introduced.

As it turned out, the programme was an immediate sensation, proving to be an antidote to all the hard news. As a result the BBC decided to continue the programme in a new mid-morning slot, and that was the beginning of Radio Ulster and a whole new area of broadcasting in Northern Ireland. Once again I found myself in the right place at the right time, and I was asked to become the sole presenter. We called it 'A Taste of Hunni', probably one of the worst puns in the business. The new format was a two-and-a-half-hour programme five days a week. Now I really had to live up to my reputation as the girl 'never short of a word'.

I immediately found myself wearing half a dozen hats, becoming disc jockey, reporter, interviewer, game show host, even auctioneer. Our range of subjects ran the spectrum from bombs, bullets and barricades to the shortage of public loos in Belfast. An over-the-airwaves second-hand shop proved highly popular, as did a type of Trivial Pursuit; ring-in competitions and 'Funny Photo' contests were also a major draw. Come to think of it, photographs on the radio was a pretty silly thing to attempt, but not as silly as the karate expert who cracked his head open trying to break a pile of bricks, or, on a different day, the illusionist sawing me in half with a chainsaw – we could have been using any sound effect from the library. We took particular pride in hosting community service projects, with a weekly spot focusing on handicapped people. One such project was to establish a guide dog fund. Listeners sent in Green Shield stamps to the tune of several thousand pounds – more than enough to train some seven guide dogs.

Guests on the show included professionals from every field imaginable: doctors, artists and educators as well as bottle collectors, herbalists and even my personal hairdresser. The programme also gave me my first real taste of celebrity chat as well. I talked by phone with singer Andy Williams, Telly 'Kojak' Savalas, and even President Jimmy Carter's mother, Miz Lillian.

'A Taste of Hunni' eventually went worldwide, featuring Irish music of all kinds. As I sat in the Belfast studio it struck me as funny to think of people in the bush in darkest Africa listening to this pot-pourri of Irish jigs and reels. I loved receiving letters from all over the world, particularly the one from a great fan in India who clearly loved the music and said, 'You'll always be assured of a bed in Bombay.'

James Galway, the Irish flautist, was due to make an appearance on the programme, but sadly was involved in a catastrophic accident when he was run down by a motorcycle, incurring multiple fractures of one arm and both legs. As he couldn't come to me, I went to him in Switzerland. I found him lying on a hospital bed, in traction and covered in plaster casts, with a huge steel frame over his body to take the weight of the bedclothes.

When I got there he made me open the wardrobe in his room and there was his collection of gold and platinum flutes glinting in this somewhat dingy ward. He could do without many things, but he wouldn't be parted from his precious flutes. The tin whistle, though, was much closer to the bed – I swear he kept it under his pillow.

That's one of the qualities I adore about him – on one hand he's the world's top flautist, and on the other he's this mischievous Ulster man who'll play a jig at the drop of a hat. He's in his element when he teams up with Paddy Maloney and The Chieftains to have a bit of a hooley on stage – a man who never forgets his roots.

James grew up in the docks area of Belfast. His father was a shipyard worker and his mother worked in a mill, but both parents were accomplished musicians: his father played the flute, fiddle and accordion and his mother played the piano. James' father began to teach his son the fiddle, but the young James discarded it for the tin whistle and then the flute. Much of his experience was picked up on the streets of Belfast with the marching bands, but eventually his talent was recognised and nurtured by musical director Douglas Dawn and his wife Muriel, and James ended up going to the Royal College of Music in London – a culture shock for this Belfast lad.

James then moved on to the prestigious Paris Conservatory, after which he began his professional career at Sadler's Wells Opera and the Royal Opera House at Covent Garden. But there was still something of the Irish rebel in him, and this was never more evident than when he was asked to audition for the Berlin Philharmonic under Herbert Von Karajan. There was a mix-up about his audition time – Von Karajan thought James was late and wasn't going to let him go through with the audition. James was having none of this: 'Look, I've travelled all this way, the time mistake is not my fault and I demand to be allowed to do the audition.' Von Karajan really put him through his paces, but there was nothing he threw at James that the talented flautist couldn't cope with. Eventually Von Karajan offered him the job as principal flautist, to which James replied, 'Well, I'll have to think about it – I'm not so sure I want the job!'

When James told his mother that he was going to take up this much coveted position and go to live in Germany, she thought he was mad and wanted him to go back to Belfast and get a proper job with the BBC.

Von Karajan was even more astonished years later when James said he was going 'solo' – after all, no one ever *left* the Berlin Philharmonic – but this Belfast kid from the docks went on to conquer the world as the man with the golden flute. He is regarded as one of Ulster's sons, and I always look forward to our interviews, which have been done everywhere over the years; from the hospital beds to hotel rooms; from dressing rooms to airports; and, probably the most memorable, the back of a black taxi en route from the Festival Hall to his hotel.

He always says, 'Come on, Glo, we Ulster people will show 'em', and the tin whistle comes out of the pocket yet again.

Of all the famous and accomplished guests on the show it is the remarkable story of one humble man that really stands out. Seventy-four-year-old Willie McElroy, born and raised in a remote area of County Fermanagh in Northern Ireland, was a humble labourer who possessed tremendous skill at singing and dancing authentic Irish jigs, a vanishing art. Willie had been performing his act in pubs and halls for nearly fifty years before folk singer Bobby Hanvey discovered him and decided to record him. Having lived in a really isolated area, Willie had spent his entire life without electricity and had never once seen television. In fact, the only time he'd ever been to Belfast was back in 1918 when horse and buggy was still the accepted mode of transportation.

To Willie, entering the electronic maze of the BBC was like finding himself in a science fiction film – or would've been if he'd ever seen one. He'd never been in a lift before and when the great oak doors opened, his jaw fell as if he was boarding a spaceship to the moon. I took him to the canteen where he ate everything in sight and marvelled, 'This is some grand hotel you've got here!'

I found him absolutely charming during our interview. 'You're a powerful fine-looking girl and a fine talker too,' he boldly flirted with me right on the air. I don't think he had any conception of mass media and couldn't believe he was being heard as far off as Scotland.

Following the spot, everyone watched in great anticipation as Willie joined Barry Cowan for a television interview on 'Scene Around Six'. It was recorded on tape and was thus immediately available for replay. When the engineer ran it back, Willie was given a chair in front of a large television screen. The look on his face as he watched himself for the first time was a mixture of sheer exhilaration and spellbinding wonder. He jumped out of his chair and scrambled up to the screen, examining it from every angle. This was one of the special moments I'll never forget. Willie McElroy found himself, at seventy-four, a recording star with a new life and career. And along the way he had discovered the twentieth century.

Perhaps my worst gaffe on air of all time happened during the run of 'Hunni'. I was rushing to the studio with my arms full of records for the next day's programme (I had to do everything myself in those days as I didn't have the luxury of a music producer). Crossing the street, I slipped on the curb and tore several ligaments in my leg. As a result I was forced to hobble about for a time on a crutch. In the snug broadcast studio it was my custom to store my chosen records for the day on the floor to my left. On this particular morning I had laid my crutch on top of the pile. Caught up in the excitement of announcing a major contest winner, I exclaimed, 'Congratulations, Mrs Jones, you've just won £150, isn't that fantastic! The only problem is you should see my poor producer grovelling under my crotch looking for the next record.'

Behind the glass I saw my engineer explode into a fit of laughter, just as I realised my terrible faux pas. 'Oh no, no. I meant my *crutch*. C-R-U-T-C-H!' I spent a good ten minutes trying to get out of that one, but the harder I tried, the worse it got.

7

Happy Days

Marnabrae Park – all £2,800 of it – formed ten years of a tapestry of family life. Paul and Michael were born while we lived there – Don was promoted from a cameraman to a director/producer and a very good one he was at that. The house backed on to farmland owned by the Boomer family and the children had a wonderful time playing on the farm – in the hay shed, milking the cows, feeding the chickens and collecting the eggs. Paul had a great trick of playing his trumpet out through the bedroom window. The cows obviously appreciated it because they came from acres away, all standing round like a bemused audience.

When Michael was born, Caron and Paul shared a tiny bedroom for a while. It was so small it always looked untidy. One day I smelt burning, checked my cooking, but discovered the smoke was coming from their bedroom. So tidy were they that a T-shirt had been chucked over a lamp and had caught fire. Fortunately only the lampshade and the T-shirt were affected.

Above: My favourite photograph of my parents

Left: Me, 6 or 7 months, appetite just as good then as it is now

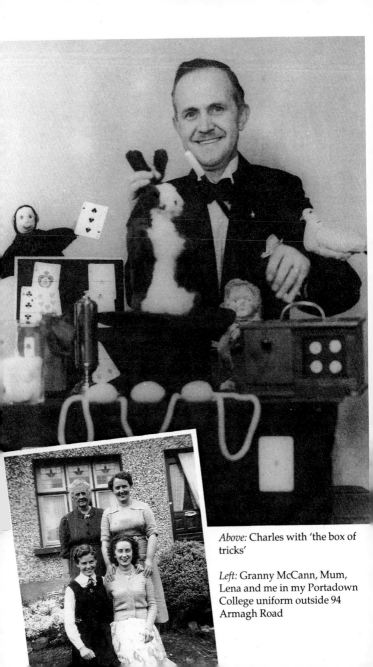

Above: Charles with 'the box of tricks'

Left: Granny McCann, Mum, Lena and me in my Portadown College uniform outside 94 Armagh Road

Top: Happy days on the hayshift

Above right: My brother Charles as a boy

Above left: Lena as guide captain and blue tit patrol, me on the right

Top: Granny and Grandad Hunniford, with my Aunt May on the left, and Aunt Myrtle, who made my stage costumes on the right

Middle: Age 6 at primary school – Mum had spent hours tonging the curls; and age 9 in my first stage frock

Left: Dad hard at work on the ads

Left: First holiday apart from my parents, with schoolfriend Margaret Doran, in Portrush

Below left: Spanking new bike – I paid Dad back at 2/6d a week

Below: A dance at Portadown College with Desi Allister, my first serious boyfriend

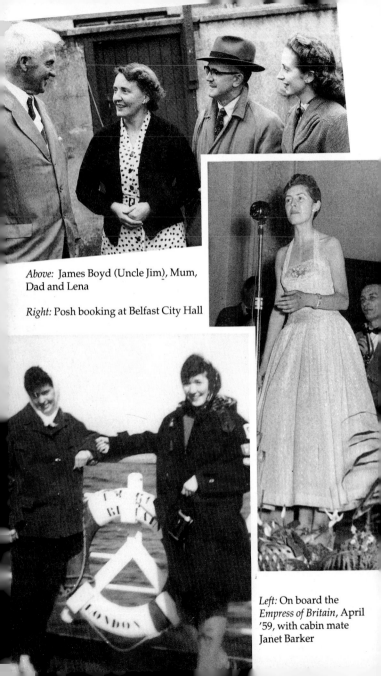

Above: James Boyd (Uncle Jim), Mum, Dad and Lena

Right: Posh booking at Belfast City Hall

Left: On board the *Empress of Britain*, April '59, with cabin mate Janet Barker

Left: The Royal Military College, Kingston, cheer leaders – me on top!

Below left: The Parade Square of Old Fort Henry, Kingston, Canada

Below: On the chair the Queen sat on during her visit to Old Fort Henry, Canada, June 1959

Above: My wedding day, 28th April 1951. Please note the 22" waist

Left: John Scholz Conway, Don and Mike Kent

The kitchen in Marnabrae was also the scene for the first commercial I ever did. Remember 'A proper cup of tea – Lyons Green Label of course'? Caron was in the high chair and I was the exhausted mother, gasping for a proper cup of tea – what drama! This was a huge date on the horizon even if I was only being paid about ten pounds. I had been warned there would be a few members of the crew arriving early in the morning. The big day dawned and at eight o'clock sharp there was a knock on the door. Three huge containers of equipment and generators were parked in the roadway. Hundreds of feet of cable had to be laid up to the house. There was a crew of about twenty-six and a thirty-five millimetre film camera, the huge lens of which, totally filled the doorway of our kitchen. The neighbours thought Hollywood had arrived in Lisburn. How disappointed they must have been to discover all those hours of rigging and shooting culminated in a thirty second commercial.

I seem to have roped the children in quite a bit for ads. Caron, though only one and a half, was totally coy and upset at making her first nude appearance in a gas commercial. The idea was she would step out of a bath into lovely warm towels, in a well heated room – a cosy scene for a gas commercial. It took much coaxing and bribing to get the ad done and I don't think she's forgiven me to this day. Paul was used in a supermarket commercial when he was just about a year old. Caron was jealous because the crew filled the trolley he was sitting in with lots of toys. One ad where the children definitely weren't needed was for sherry. After yours truly had sipped her way through thirty-five takes I could have been anywhere.

Back to more sobering thoughts, the house in Marnabrae was getting a bit cramped for three growing children and as my job was picking up speed alongside Don's new position, we decided to move to Hillsborough, a beautiful village about fourteen miles south of Belfast. We found a four bedroom bungalow standing in three quarters of an acre of land. It was just outside the village and it felt decidedly grand. We knew there would be other houses built around eventually, but that didn't stop us making the most of being surrounded by lush green fields divided by high hedges bulging in the springtime with pink and white may flower blossom.

Hillsborough Village is basically one long rather wide street culminating in a hill at the top. It is the location for Government House, the Queen's official residence in Northern Ireland. It was given its name by Lord Arthur Hill and I have often sung (and indeed recorded) a song very much identified with the village called 'In the Gloaming' (not to be confused with 'Roaming in the Gloaming'). It is the story of Annie Fortescue Harrison who came to the village, met and fell madly in love with Lord Arthur Hill. He was married at the time so their love couldn't be. Years later he heard a beautiful song, inquired who had written it and discovered it was the aforementioned Annie.

> In the gloaming oh my darling
> When the lights are dim and low
> And the quiet shadows falling
> Softly come and softly go
> When the winds are sighing faintly
> With a gentle unknown woe
> Will you think of me and love me
> As you did once long ago
> In the gloaming oh my darling

Think not bitterly of me
Though I passed away in silence
Left you lonely, left you free
For my heart was crushed with longing
What had been could never be
It was best to leave you thus dear
Best for you and best for me

I'm glad to say this story had a happy ending because eventually when his first wife died Lord Arthur Hill met up with Annie Fortescue Harrison and they lived happily ever after. A few years back when Sir Harry Secombe went to Hillsborough for his programme 'Highway' I had the pleasure of singing the song inside Government House in one of the magnificent drawing rooms.

There was one occasion when I wasn't so welcome at Government House. Jeanette Charles, the woman who makes a good living as a look-alike for the Queen, was a guest on our 'Good Evening Ulster' show. Stanley Matchett, a photographer with the *Daily Mirror*, thought it would make a great picture to have Jeanette in all her regalia at the gates of Government House with the secretary – custodian of the house in the Queen's absence, to meet her officially. Not only did he agree to the ruse but he said 'Ma'am, so pleased you could make it, please come inside.' We took the photographs from the driveway and Stanley was thrilled with his exclusive, but later in the day he had a call from the secretary, who had been given a rollicking from his wife for having agreed to such a tasteless stunt. So the photographs were pulled and Stanley lost his scoop.

We quickly settled into life in Hillsborough. Being a country girl at heart I loved the then rural setting with the convenience of a friendly and pretty village on the door-step. Even our golden labrador 'Che' got the hang of it. He would leave the house in the morning, call for his pooch friend at the pottery in the village (belonging to Chris Patten) and off they would go for a walk around the lake in the forest at the other end of the village. Eventually Che would amble home, happy but exhausted. Everyone in the village knew him and he collected many bones and titbits from the shops along the way. Eventually when we moved to Sevenoaks, Che thought he could do the same thing but with such law abiding citizens around he would only have to escape from our fenceless garden for two minutes when he would be reported to the police. I seemed to spend a lot of my first six months in England either in the police station or apologising to my neigh-bours Mary and Geoff Day for a wandering labrador who seemed very partial to their bins! One day in Hillsborough I called in to see my friend Bertie in the antique shop who took great glee in telling me that the previous day he had taken a customer upstairs to see his antique four-poster bed, beautifully fitted out with expensive drapes and matching bedding, only to discover Che lying in the bed, head slumped across the pillows.

Such was the simple life in County Down.

Not all of it was sweetness and light. Paul, now about thirteen years old, had made friends with a neighbour's boy, Michael Shiels, who lived across the road in the middle of eight acres, including a lake. One dark rainy night his Mum Diane was driving up the long lonely lane to the house when suddenly a man dropped out of the trees on to the car bonnet. Of course she was absolutely terrified, but it transpired that the sinister man was actually a life-size dummy, made by Paul and Michael, and dressed in their dad's clothes. At a time of trouble and strife in Northern Ireland, the boys were not popular in the Shiels' household for a while, and I don't think Diane's blood pressure recovered too quickly.

It was from Hillsborough that I was now doing my daily dash to Belfast. What had started out as a part-time freelance job was now more than full time, so I just loved my weekends at home. On Sunday mornings I could hardly wait for Don to leave to play golf, then my friend Anne would come up for our weekly dose of coffee and chat. Having spent all those years as neighbours in Lisburn, we had so much to catch up on: who had I met during the week, how were things at the Royal Victoria Hospital where Billy and Anne worked . . . We bared our souls to each other, and of course, because Anne and her husband were both medical, they got all the questions about ailments, from migraines to cuts and bruises, from eating habits to potty training.

One day I got a call which was to have me screeching down the phone to Anne straight away. I had been for a routine smear test and the results had come back showing decidedly dodgy cells. What did it mean? I wept. Was it inevitable I had cancer, and would I have to be operated on? Anne had all the questions fired at her fast and furiously. I was later taken into hospital where they zapped whatever they had to by laser, and, thank God, the subsequent smears were clear. As Anne pointed out, 'At least now you will be checked very regularly', and thankfully all has been fine ever since.

Not all our time was to be spent at Hillsborough. Don and I took the kids on weekends to County Fermanagh on the west coast of Northern Ireland where we rented a cottage on Lord Erne's Crom Castle estate. He had decided to move all his staff from what was known as the 'piggeries' up into the stable yard and build them cosy apartments with central heating. All the old cottages that remained in the piggeries he put on the market to be rented out. We joined the company of the city slickers who hopped into the car to spend rustic weekends in cottages that cost an absurdly meagre £135 per year.

The idea of the nominal fee was that the renters would make a few improvements during their stay. We chose an immense stone double-fronted house on the edge of a twelve-foot deep lough where the fishing was so good it was said to contain 'ten foot of fish and two of water'. Legend had it that one should stay away at Easter because the lough would inevitably claim lives. It did seem that every Easter holiday there would invariably be some sort of boating accident.

Folklore aside, it was an idyllic place for the children to grow up, with its 2,500 acres they could roam about in. Paul had the choice of a new bicycle or a second-hand mini-car and chose the latter, learning to drive at about ten years of age on the estate. Lord Erne's daughter was selling off her pony, Brandy, which we bought for Caron along with the year's grazing rights at fifty quid.

One year Don and I went for a short holiday in Dublin and left the kids with their babysitter on the estate. Apparently our dog Jip escaped from the farmyard and killed two pheasants. Lord Erne stomped into the farmyard bearing the two birds and shouting furiously, 'Gloria's dog did this! I'm gonna shoot the bugger if he ever does it again.'

We had some wonderful times in our five years at Fermanagh. Sometimes Lord Erne let us go up to the castle and swim in the conservatory pool. We fished in the lake and had communal barbecues in the courtyard with the other families. I remember there was an old smuggler's fishing boat we used to take up the river and across the border. It was the leakiest craft you ever saw with just a tiny motor and yet we all piled in, bailing as we went. Coming back in the dark the boat was barely an inch out of the water. No one had life jackets and few of us could swim. The kids remember those days as fabulous times but I shudder to recall how irresponsible Don and I were at times. We were having too good a time to notice.

Lord Erne, who lives at Crom Castle and works the estate, is a firm believer in leprechauns. Indeed he insists such a being is the custodian of Crom Castle. It seems the original castle burnt down and had to be re-sited. As re-building got under way, the workmen began to put up the walls, only to find, the next day, that their work had been flattened overnight. So the building was re-sited yet again. Just as mysteriously, all the silver disappeared from the Castle, and was never recovered. Lord Erne claims to know where it lies but, the story goes, anyone trying to defy providence by recovering the booty will be robbed of their eldest child. When someone did attempt to dig it up, his dog keeled over on the spot. The mystery of the missing silver remains unsolved to this day.

Even today some of the Irish maintain a healthy respect for these magical beings, remembering to leave a mound of dirt for the fairies when they dig for turf. Fairies are said to alight in blackthorn trees and even today no one would ever think to cut one down. Even if one were in the middle of a proposed roadway, the planners would never disturb it, but think of a way to make a detour round it.

The Irish are a superstitious lot. Not even green is always considered lucky. My mother would never have green carpeting or green clothes in the house. Typical of the Irish, she had a host of superstitions she faithfully abided by, many associated with death. For instance, if a picture fell off the wall for no reason, you were sure to hear of a loved one dying and she always said things happened in threes. Another was if you heard the cry of the banshee, the cloaked woman, death would soon be near. I used to imagine I heard the cry – it was probably only cats in the night. But as a child I was terrified I'd see the banshee in our street. The oddest one she faithfully observed was called 'Saturday flit, short sit'. She'd always say, 'Never move house on a Saturday or else you'll only have a short time there.' Mum would carry this to extremes. When she was in hospital for an operation she was due to be released on a Saturday, but she simply wouldn't have it. Finally we told her, 'Mum, this is silly. Why spend another twenty-four hours in a hospital when you could be home?' She grudgingly gave in and oddly she was back in hospital the following Tuesday with complications of phlebitis.

She so instilled this in me that after a tennis accident I too put off being discharged on a Saturday and waited until the next day to go home. In fact, I have retained many of these superstitions. Another practice I follow is never putting shoes on a table, and if I drop a glove I won't pick it up myself. If someone else picks it up I never say thank you. And as for Friday the 13th, I'd rather not even think about it.

Caron and I both have 'lucky clothes'. This started

when I was a child: whenever I wore my yellow taffeta I would invariably win a prize or contest. I still associate certain clothes or jewellery with things working well for me.

It's not just the Irish who are superstitious. When I interviewed Nana Mouskouri she told me she always enters the stage from the left side, and she must have the same handkerchief on stage with her every time she sings. The great Pavarotti has to find a rusty nail to bring him luck before a performance, so his sidekicks scatter them between his dressing room and the stage prior to his appearance.

On weekends when we weren't down at the cottage I tried to give the kids a full range of recreational experiences. Admittedly, there's a certain guilt factor built into working mothers for which we desperately try to compensate. For a while I was on a cultural outings kick. Every weekend I made sure they all attended a play, or a musical, museum or gallery, seeking to hone their education in fine arts.

And then there was the odd short holiday, like the time we were determined to spend a few days at the beach. Typical of Irish weather it blew up quite a gale, yet like fools Don and I bullishly insisted we all have a good time, trying to build sand castles as the rain and wind kicked up great walls of water.

Speaking of the water, I never learned to swim. Back in Portadown our school didn't have a pool. No one we knew had one and even going down to Newcastle in County Down, the sea was enough to turn you blue from head to toe. The only pool we had regular access to was a filthy pond outside a factory some ten miles away from school. We'd be taken on the bus once a month to this icy pond infested with dirty leaves and be expected to swim.

The only occasion when we could really enjoy the water was during our one big day out every year for our Sunday school trip. We went on the steam train to Bangor, about thirty-five miles away. We each had about five shillings – a fortune in those days – the idea being to spend all the money while we were there. For the big occasion Mum used to curl my hair either by setting it in rags or fashioning ringlets from tongs heated over a gas flame. I was standing at the edge of the water at Picky Pool watching everyone when someone came running up behind and pushed me in. People often talk about going down for the third time. Well, I was right under for what seemed a petrified eternity. Onlookers thought I was just playing around but luckily for me I was fished out in the nick of time. I had to stand around the remainder of the day soaking wet, my hair bedraggled, in a state of shock.

To this day I'm terrified of the water and Caron insists I instilled my own fear into her and her brothers. Although I desperately wanted them to learn to swim I wouldn't allow them to venture into the deep end, wouldn't let them dive off the board. 'You can learn to swim,' I'd tell them, 'but stay in the shallow end. You can swim just as well in three feet as you can in six.'

My fears were reinforced by an alarming experience Paul had as a child. He was playing by the steps in the shallow end, then I looked up from my reading to see him floating head down in the water. I screamed across the pool and ran round the side just as a man dragged him out. We had to thump his back and force water from his lungs to bring him round. I'd never seen anyone look so pale and drained. Paul, like me, has a terrible dread of the water and it's only in recent years that he's learned to swim.

Every time I interview Rolf Harris he says he could teach me to swim in one day . . . and he should know because he was a champion swimmer in Australia.

A more pleasant memory of weekends in Hillsborough is our Saturday routine. While Don was out golfing, the kids and I would go shopping in the morning and bring back a heavenly Swiss chocolate cake absolutely oozing with cream. We'd brew a pot of tea and settle down before the television with a fire roaring and spend the afternoon watching old movies. These were the films I grew up on, the romantic *Breakfast At Tiffany's*, *An Affair to Remember* and *From Here to Eternity* and all those enduring Hollywood musicals. Caron still talks about those afternoons as some of her most treasured childhood memories.

Although the children were fast growing up as the seventies wore on, I still managed to fit my work schedule round family life. Throughout my travels, whether it was going on location to film a show from Scotland or a trip to London, I would come home with a doll for Caron's vast collection. She had shelves and shelves of them. Then I would sit up nights, sometimes until 3:00 am, knitting or sewing outfits for them, so as soon as she opened her eyes in the morning she would find a newly dressed doll at the foot of her bed to add to her brood.

Like all children, mine certainly had their share of unhappy incidents. One day I had a message at work to say that Caron had cut her face at school. So I jumped straight into my car, the tears streaming down my face, wondering if she was going to be scarred for life. She'd been peering over some railings in the playground, slipped and become impaled on a railing. They had to lift her off the railing. By the time I arrived at the hospital she'd been stitched up. If it had been a fraction of an inch one way the railing would have pierced her jugular. Luckily for her the young doctor on duty that day did a brilliant job sewing her up, and the scar is almost unnoticeable.

Paul was heavily into sports. In fact, he was an outstanding runner. He had a very unconventional style, putting his heels down first, and the coaches tried desperately to change his form until Paul gave it up altogether. He was also a member of his school's rugby team. One day he didn't show up for a match, and by the time I found out about it I was absolutely incensed. He'd let his team down, which is something I cannot abide. When you commit yourself to a project, you're honour bound to keep your word.

I confronted Paul while I was doing the dishes that night, unleashing a tirade of fury: 'Where were you? Why didn't you turn up? How dare you do this!' Whatever he tried to say in his own defence only served to enrage me all the more. I took a cup I'd been drying and hurled it at him. He, of course, ducked and the cup smashed against the wall. 'Now look what you've done to my good cup!' I screamed. The climax of the incident had me picking up a breadboard and chasing him all over the house, hurling abuse. It was one of my rare extremes of discipline and still goes down as one of the more memorable Keating family stories.

Michael once returned from a boating trip blonder than I am. He'd gone off with mousy coloured hair and come back peroxide blond. So I had to pack him off to the hairdressers because he couldn't go back to school looking as he did.

If I've come down hard on the children for anything, it's been drugs. When I was a child drugs weren't a problem and I determined that my kids would never so much as touch them. The kids find it strange that I've never been exposed to drugs. I personally have never taken anything. The closest I came to it was in 1978 at Studios in Dublin where I was recording an album called 'A Taste of Hunni'. As I was listening to a playback, the musical director came through and said, 'Hi darling, do you want a ciggy?'

In my puritan way I quickly replied, 'Oh no, no. I never smoke, thank you very much.'

'Oh no,' he smirked, 'I meant a *real* ciggy.'

I was shocked as I watched the reefer being passed round the technical people. For a brief moment I was tempted to take a puff, but I was simply too terrified.

The incident sparked off memories of friends of my parents who lived in Dundalk, just over the border in the south of Ireland. I loved going down by train for the odd holiday. When I was twelve I received one of those wildly expensive trench coats for Christmas and teamed with my sharp white mohair scarf this was one of my first truly adult looks. My hosts had a nine-year-old daughter whom I took aside and slyly suggested, 'Why don't we go over to the shop across the street and pretend we're getting cigarettes for your granny?'

Over we tramped and I boldly spoke up to the clerk: 'Mrs Coburn would like five Woodbine, please.' Stores were not allowed to sell cigarettes to minors and the shopkeeper knew Mrs Coburn would never smoke Woodbine, but nonetheless we were able to buy the pack. My young companion and I stole back to the house where we lit up two cigarettes, coughed and gagged and decided we hated the things. I pushed the packet into my coat pocket and we breezed into the sitting room as though nothing had happened. But the sharp-eyed mother didn't miss a thing. 'You girls weren't smoking or anything today, were you?'

My heartbeat quickened. 'Oh, no, certainly not,' I said a little too airily. 'What a silly old thing to say.'

'I swear I smelled it round the house.'

I made the stupid mistake of pulling my belt out of my coat and out spilled the three remaining ciggies right in front of the family. My face flushed a glowing red, caught in the lie. I was mortified.

It obviously did the trick, because to this day I'm a non-smoker. However the only real urge to smoke I've experienced was during my three pregnancies – if anyone left a packet lying around I couldn't resist the temptation to pick it up.

As my family before, we've always been a close lot and I could never bear to be separated from the kids. One of the worst times was when Caron left for France when she was seventeen, to become an au pair. The night before she left we both cried the entire time. I couldn't bear seeing her get on the plane in London. I suddenly knew how my mother must have felt all those years ago as I left home for Canada at the same age. I impulsively shoved Michael in the car, dashed to Dover, got on a ferry and drove as near to Paris as I could.

Looking back on it Caron remembers: 'Before Mum had to finally turn back she telephoned me and said, "I just want you to know that we're close. You're not alone. We're thinking about you." I thought that was brilliant.'

It turned out Caron only stuck the job for three weeks. After that she went to Paris and had a ball. So much for me worrying about her being homesick!

In 1979 I was rolling along doing my daily radio programme, 'A Taste of Hunni' when Ulster Television got in
touch. They had decided to embark on a revolutionary
path with their six o'clock news programme. Up until that
point they had been broadcasting a format of total hard
news. Suddenly the producers decided viewers were fed
up with violence and destruction night after night so they
resolved to give the news exactly the amount of time it
was worth. If it was a soft day in terms of hard-hitting
events it would get ten minutes of an hourly programme;
a newsier day would dictate maybe thirty-five minutes.
However, the rest of the hour would be filled with maga-
zine-type pieces, celebrity profiles and community
events, even competitions. They wanted me to become
the programme's main presenter.

Even as I accepted I never dreamed I would work so
hard. It was the most formative time in my working life.
Not a day goes by when I don't think back to that discipline. Not only was I presenting 'Good Evening, Ulster',
but I was also assistant producer. Along with the producer Alan Wright, a Londoner of great enthusiasm and
inspiration, I dreamed up the items, researched the
stories and went out in the mornings to shoot them. Then
I'd come back and have to edit the film myself, write the
script and get the rest of the programme ready, apart from
the news, which was put together by a very efficient news
room. It was always a flurry of last-minute changes,
coupled with finding the right clothes and make-up.
Sometimes I'd be gone all day, not getting home until
eight or nine at night. Looking back I have no idea how
we all kept up the pace day after day. But it was an immense success, sitting securely in the top ten programmes
all five nights. Before we started the programme I went

round all the publicity people and agents and record companies in London, asking them to bear us in mind for celebrity guests. Two people were particularly helpful, John Howson from Polydor, and the publicity man Clifford Elson.

The Belfast BBC news team had been totally scathing of our experiment. 'It'll never work,' they chided. 'Imagine all this devastation going on and they're going to come out of the news and go to some pop star.' But they had to eat their words. This new format captured the imagination of the public and proved that the audience was relieved to hear some good news for a change and to find out what else was going on in the province. On top of it all, I was in competition with Don who by this stage was directing the rival BBC evening news programme – so we always had a lot to talk about.

Luckily he was able to get away earlier than me to look after the children. Caron, now in her teens, helped out considerably, picking up Michael from school and pitching in with the chores. We were also blessed with our trusted babysitter Gillie and her husband, Tom, whom the children called 'Papa'. They were almost like grandparents to the children. There were some who criticised me for not being a stay-at-home Mum. I used to feel guilty, not merely about working, but actually liking my job. Years back, people weren't supposed to enjoy work; rather, it was meant to be something you did for money. The professionals now say it's better to have a woman who is fulfilled and happy, than a woman who stays at home completely frustrated and unhappy. When I asked the kids about it – would they rather I were a more traditional mother – they resoundingly answered, 'No!'

In the middle of these discussions, Paul has said, 'I

can't think of one deficiency any of us suffered because Mum's professional life had taken over. I think she tries to be everything and even *more* than a mother can be. Years later when I was laid up with a hernia operation she was ready to cancel all her engagements to look after me.'

The fact is that the kids always found my world exciting and wanted to be part of it. It was a great way of keeping us all together.

Particularly interesting was the opportunity to meet full-blown celebrities. On my past programme I'd interviewed the odd star, but with a handful of exceptions never the really big international names. Previously, Ulster Television had maintained a policy of airing interviews with celebrities only if they were tied to an appearance they were making in the area via a play or concert, or if they'd written a book. We changed that policy, reasoning, 'Why do you need an excuse to interview someone? A name is a name.'

Suddenly everyone was coming on the programme: Jean Michael Jarre, Charlotte Rampling and Bob Geldof, Billy Connolly, Dick Emery. Not that we didn't have to bow and scrape to get the big names. Because of all the troubles, stars were reluctant to come to Northern Ireland, so when they did, it was a monumental event.

On one occasion Elton John was appearing in Belfast for a concert. We tried every which way – promoters, agents, personal assistants – to get him to come on the programme. I even sent flowers to his hotel room and used my contacts with managers of local hotels to put in a word for us, but nothing worked. Finally after days and days of trying, out of the blue we received a phone call at five o'clock. 'If you come round to the hotel at half six, I'll do the interview,' he agreed. The only problem was we were on the air at that time. Still, I couldn't let this stellar opportunity slide by.

I presented the show until twenty past six and then said on air, 'I've got to leave now as I'm off to do an interview with Elton John, which we'll have for you tomorrow night,' and quite unconventionally left the show in the hands of my co-presenter Gerry Kelly, who is now one of the biggest celebrities in Ireland. I showed up at the Europa in the centre of Belfast, the one famous for having been blown up over thirty times.

The interview went well. Elton said, 'I'm really sorry we didn't go into the studio.'

Picking up on his accessibility I quickly countered, 'Well look, we've done this great piece now, why don't we do a really big special and have you live in the studio tomorrow night so you can take phone calls from people?'

'Yeah, I think I'd like that,' he nodded. 'It's be nice to talk to some of the young people of Northern Ireland.'

The next night we pulled our fabulous surprise. 'And now after this commercial break we'll have Elton John live in the studio to take your calls.' Needless to say, the entire switchboard practically collapsed under the strain of eager fans trying to dial in. After the phone session, which Elton found extremely enjoyable, fans collected outside from all over the area and in their enthusiasm pushed in a window of his car just as he had got in and was about to be driven away. Elton, the glass coming down on him, was visibly shaken at being in a crowd scene in Belfast, of all places, during a particularly violent stage of the troubles.

On another occasion, singer Van Morrison, a Belfast native, came on the programme. He hadn't been back to Ulster in years to perform and the concert sold out in something like twenty minutes. We did the interview downtheline from London. When we cut across to London Van was sitting in a chair with his feet up on a table, drinking a cup of tea and munching biscuits. He did the whole interview slurping his tea and picking bits of cracker from his teeth. People still talk about that interview. Besides being incredibly rude, one of the world's finest singer-songwriters muttered nothing but 'yeahs' and 'yups' throughout the interview – not the best piece of live television.

Throughout my career I'm amazed at how many interviews we've been able to get through default or sheer innocence. I often bypassed the proper channels and went straight to the top, to bosses or even celebs themselves, to ask for an interview, working on the adage they can only say 'no'. Usually it's climbing through that frustrating net of managers and publicity people that's the toughest part. Once you break through to the celebrity himself he or she is normally glad to give you a bit of their time.

Following my earlier contacts with Polydor, I had a call one day from John Howson saying 'How would you like to do an interview with Donny and Marie Osmond?'

This was the absolute heyday of the Osmond Family worldwide. We flew to London to record the interview on a Saturday morning and by the time it was seen on Monday night it was the talk of Northern Ireland – Donny and Marie being on Ulster Television.

Now that 'Good Evening, Ulster' was regularly nabbing the big names, a whole new world opened up for my kids. Suddenly they were pleading to come down to the station or to do their homework in my dressing room for a chance to meet their favourite stars.

Caron in particular remembers this as an exciting period: 'When Mum started doing television we could go to school the next morning and say we'd met Elton John or whoever the pop star of the moment was. All our friends would be green.

'There was always something different happening and I think that was why I decided to go into television myself. Also, going round with Mum as we did, we quickly learned to develop social skills. When you're with a celebrity you soon learn that people are only interested in talking to that person. If you're in their wake you just get tossed to one side. So very early on my brothers and I decided that we could either go and sit quietly like wall-flowers or talk to people independently. We did the latter.'

Paul always viewed it as a major advantage: 'Through Mum's job I've met quite a few famous people and it's made it easier today, as now I don't get excited meeting any big names and I can talk to people. You see these people for what they are, just regular, normal guys. They're all human beings just like anyone else.'

Michael was still at an age when just being around the set was an adventure. He would walk over to the studios from school and have a rousing time running about the corridors meeting fascinating people.

'Ulster Television was such a friendly atmosphere,' he recalls. 'If Mum was in the middle of an interview I'd often go up and interrupt and say to the guest, "Sir, can you help me with this spelling?" One night they were live on air and I went up to get some help with my French homework. As I was walking across the set, suddenly this arm grabbed me and I was behind the weather-board. Here's the weather lady on the other side doing the weather live to the nation and I'm standing behind there chatting to Mum, "How do I say this in French?" It was that wonderful sort of atmosphere I'll never forget.'

Michael also remembers the night we had Rod Stewart on the show in his infamous leopard-skin tights. It was a prerecorded interview as Rod was playing Dublin that night. The moment we went off air at seven, I rounded up all the kids in the car and we raced down to the venue to see Stewart in concert.

Even my own mother got caught up in all the celebrity hoopla. Although she was hooked in by the panoply of star names, the one she really got wound up over was snooker champion Dennis Taylor. She would never miss a snooker game on television, especially if Dennis was playing. One night during the final of the world championship, the match was so close I couldn't bear the tension, so I hid out in the hall, asking Mum for play by play reports. The next day I interviewed Dennis about his dramatic win and he forever after teased me about my unusual way of watching snooker. In later years, when he appeared on 'Sunday Sunday', I was able to introduce him to Mum, his biggest fan. She was thrilled out of her mind, needless to say, and went home with a souvenir photograph taken together.

The experience that really stands out from my stint on 'Good Evening, Ulster' is not the Rod Stewarts or Elton Johns, but big-band leader James Last. James has the reputation of both being a gourmet and looking after the needs of his orchestra while on tour.

In 1980 he was performing in Dublin and we went to the Mirabelle restaurant to film an interview. The Mirabelle was situated outside Dublin and was owned by Sean Kinsella, who'd been a chef on board the *QE II* and *Cambra*. His menus didn't include a price list, so you never knew in advance what you had to pay. Sean would also choose the wine for you. The price was determined by whether you were on a company budget or paying for it yourself.

We went to film the party after the show and we walked into the restaurant that evening to be met with the most spectacular haute cuisine I'd ever witnessed. There were gargantuan trays piled high with Dublin Bay prawns, smoked salmon, and quantities of seafood, followed by Sean's speciality of boneless duck in a delectable sauce. This was washed down with salamanders of champagne and the best chablis, not forgetting the two crates of Château Margot that Sean had purchased at £124 per bottle. This was the fare that James Last fed his band of some seventy musicians. The bill was a staggering £17,500!

James always says that's how he keeps the same orchestra year after year – because he looks after them so well. When he subsequently came to Belfast to perform in a huge sports arena there he insisted that Sean travel with him on the bus to feed them en route in the manner to which they were accustomed.

My three years of presenting 'Good Evening, Ulster' marked a dramatic change in my everyday life. Appearing on television meant there was now a face to go with the voice. Because our format was one of easy access with the public that attitude flowed off air as well. People would come up on the street with comments ranging from, 'What was the answer to that trivia question last night?' to 'Love that dress you were wearing!' Since Northern Ireland was such a friendly place and because I'd been in the public eye since age nine, I didn't find it that difficult an adjustment. The kids will tell you, however, that it took me ages to do any shopping, since I had to stop every two minutes to chat.

As Caron tells the story, 'In the supermarkets Paul and I used to walk way behind Mum and listen to what people were saying about her, good and bad. Everyone recognised her because she was on television every day. They'd pass comment on her clothes and hair, and some women would go into the hairdressers and ask for a Gloria cut. It was frightening – she was becoming an institution.'

One thing I'm grateful for is that the kids were never teased by their classmates or made to feel alienated because of who their mother was. Of course, there was the inevitable bit of gossiping at lunch or snickering on the bus home. But more often than not, I was viewed in their eyes as the hip Mum who was interviewing Cliff Richard and knew which pop stars were in the charts better than they did. While other parents would be saying, 'Turn that rubbish off,' I'd be saying 'Turn it up!'

Those enriching, exhilarating days were tempered by some dark and difficult ones. It was in 1970 that I got a call in the middle of the night from my mother saying Dad had had his stroke. 'It's a bad one, Gloria.'

When I rushed down to the house to see Mum and Lena it was as if he had already died. The outlook for his recovery was not good. There had been a deep bleed in his brain which had paralysed him on one side and left him in a state of semi-consciousness. The doctor said it was doubtful he'd ever come out of it.

As I walked into his hospital room he was in a cot

with the rails up to keep him from falling out of bed. The worst part was seeing the blank, disorientated stare in his eyes. I realised he didn't even recognise me. I tried to will him to smile, to say my name, to take my hand like I knew he wanted to somewhere deep inside. I couldn't come to terms with our eyes making contact, knowing that this was my Dad, yet knowing too that he might never be the same again.

But there was a spark of the old fight in him – a tough 'wee nut' as we would say in Northern Ireland. When the nurse came in to feed him he'd muster what little strength he had and brush her aside. Systematically, as the days went on, he'd push her away with more force and stubborn defiance until he reached the point where he would insist on feeding himself. We watched as Dad made progress, fighting to sit up, to keep the side of the bed down, trying to regain his dignity. After about ten days he was once again recognising us.

He amazed us with his recovery and triumphantly returned home, to our great joy. Eventually he regained some strength in his limbs and worked on his speech, which had been badly slurred. I could see the frustration on his face when he was unable to string the correct words together. He'd say something like, 'It's a hot moon today,' and beneath the immediate laughter I could read his bitter exasperation.

When someone entered the house Dad would try to pick them up to demonstrate how strong he was. I suspect that his loss of strength frightened him more than anything else and he was constantly trying to compensate which resulted in him becoming extremely demanding at times. If he wanted something he'd have to have it there and then. At mealtimes, for instance, he had to have his dinner right there and then. No waiting a half hour or even ten minutes. He would also cry very easily, becoming extremely emotional.

For me it became exceedingly difficult to watch the strong father I remembered, reduced to but a fragment of what he'd once been. Yet he retained a good quality of life. Although he suffered two or three additional strokes none was as bad as the first and he went on to live several years more.

On his seventieth birthday we sprang the most wonderful surprise. Dad thought he was coming up to Lena's to help her choose a carpet because he'd always had a good eye for colour. We all hid behind the sitting room furniture and when he came in, sprang our surprise, complete with birthday cake and candles. He adored it, eyes gleaming in childlike wonder.

Before his last Christmas in 1980 I was trying to work out what Dad would like more than anything else – and I decided it was my brother Charles. He works in computer graphics in Staffordshire. I went to the airport to collect Charles along with his wife Libby and their two children, Kerry and Michael, hid them in the car and then prepared Dad so he wouldn't keel over from the shock.

'Now Dad, just sit down here, I've got this big box I'm going to bring in for you,' I told him. The look on his face as they burst in to embrace him told me that I couldn't have come up with a more perfect or welcomed gift. What a Christmas we all had together in the family home in Portadown.

As Providence would have it, my timing couldn't have been better. As I kissed Dad good night, telling him how much I loved him, I had a profound feeling of satisfaction that I had tied up all the loose ends. The following year he died peacefully in his sleep.

Mum, naturally, was completely devastated. Her entire life had been her family and, especially in later years with us kids off on our own, she depended all the more on Dad. Lena and I used to come by on Saturdays to get her out of the house – Dad had been buried on a Saturday. I would invariably come into the kitchen to find her in tears as she baked his favourite bread. We had grave doubts as to whether she was strong enough to manage on her own. But in the end she did remarkably well. At first Lena stayed with her, but after a time Mum said, 'This is silly. You can't go on like this. You've got your own family.' I'm sure she must have died a thousand times over – she hated being alone as much as I do – but she got used to it as everyone has to. And she showed herself to be made of some pretty sterling stuff.

When we cleaned out Dad's things I was finally able to rummage through his magician's cupboard without fear of being found out. Surrounding myself with the tricks that were such a part of him, I longed to become his little girl again, to once more feel his strong arms lift me on to the stage, to feel his big hand warmly circling my own and to take our bows together before a roaring, beaming crowd. It's only now I realise how much I am my father's daughter.

Lena, Charles and I all have our favourite cherished mementos of Dad and mine is his treasured book of magic tricks, like the one he gave to me to record my childhood performances. I only have one real regret: he never saw me achieve the broadcasting success that was just a few short years away, the career he so enthusiastically envisioned for me, even when I didn't know it myself.

But then again, somehow, wherever he is, I think he knows.

8

Gus Honeybun

I believe in life there are chance meetings with people taking you to turning points that change your whole life. The debt of gratitude I owe my former producer in Belfast, Dan Gilbert, can never be measured, and I fully expected to find his liberal attitudes everywhere. But in other parts of the BBC network, the only voices that came wafting over the airwaves were those of men.

So in early 1979 just before I was due to start at Ulster Television, I was a bit anxious about leaving the BBC even though I was looking forward to daily television. Once again I decided to go straight to the top. I boldly rang up BBC London controllers Charles McClelland and David Hatch: 'You don't know me, but I work for BBC Northern Ireland. Is there any chance I could come in and see you for a cup of coffee?'

They were quite amenable and agreed to meet me. When you're not looking for a job and have nothing to lose, you tend to let down your guard and say things you wouldn't ordinarily. Even so, I couldn't possibly have foreseen the ramifications of our brief conversation.

'Look, I'm in the process of leaving the BBC,' I told McClelland. 'I don't know if I'm doing the right thing, but I'm committed to going to Ulster Television. So I'm not here looking for a job. But I *am* here to tell you there is a huge void on your network because there are no women.' I pushed on, gathering steam. 'You may think it's only women who are at home listening, but men certainly have car radios and listen at work. Retired men tune in at home and then there are the unemployed.'

'You're absolutely right,' he nodded. 'By the way, do you know anything about music?'

With that, I whipped out a copy of my record 'A Taste of Hunni' which I just happened to have about my person. 'Why don't I leave this with you along with my details and maybe sometime something might crop up?' I naively hoped that he might actually listen to the record, and maybe get me some air play, but I expected nothing more. I was simply grateful he'd given me the opportunity to speak my mind. That was the end of it or so I thought.

Two and a half years later in 1981 I was in London filming an interview for 'Good Evening, Ulster' when I got a call from my secretary, Ann Black. 'You've had a call from the "Jimmy Young Show". They want to know can you do two weeks holiday relief?'

I laughed out loud. 'C'mon, Ann, someone's pulling your leg. If BBC London were going to ask me to present a programme, they'd want to talk to me, audition me, find out what it is that I do, if I'm even qualified. They wouldn't just offer it out of the blue.'

'Well, here's the number and the name. I really think you should call back.'

I did just that and, incredibly, found the offer absolutely legit. Here was my big chance to do network radio, unexpectedly dropped in my lap and given to me by David Hatch, whom I'd met a few years before when I'd had the cheek to tell them what was wrong with their network! I was thrilled and somewhat in shock. I couldn't wait to tell Don and the kids. Mum would be over the moon about it. Wouldn't Dad have been proud? I thought.

And then sheer terror hit me. Forget the fact that I was jumping headfirst into network radio. Forget that Jimmy Young had the top political programme in Britain. Forget that no one even knew who the hell I was. What scared me most was the daunting, wholly intimidating notion of having to exchange witty repartee with Terry Wogan during the five-minute crossover, so legendary even the Queen listened to it. I'd interviewed Terry from Ulster and I knew this was a man who could destroy you with one swipe of that rapier tongue.

I lay in bed at night, planning my strategy, practising exchanges in my head, wondering how on earth I would begin to match this broadcasting legend tit-for-tat. I made calls to find out what was going on his life, how he was doing on the golf course, any ammunition to hit him with. It was the handover period that could break me before I even got as far as the programme. There was only one strategy: I would go on the offensive . . .

Taking my chair in the broadcast booth at Radio Two that first morning, I was so focused on escaping the Wogan jaws that I didn't have time to appreciate the fact that I was possibly setting myself up for failure before a staggering audience of eight million discerning listeners. Terry lost no time in launching in: 'Next up we have

"Grievous Bodily Hunniford". Gosh, I can see her now behind the glass, wearing those slinky fishnet stockings and high heels.'

'I'm so disappointed,' I sighed in mock exasperation. 'My grandmother's been talking about you for years. I expected some handsome man in a smart suit and here you are sitting there unshaven with egg stains down your dressing gown. Look at you, you're a disgrace!'

It not only worked, but became an instant phenomenon. The mere fact that Miss Nobody dared to cheek the great Terry Wogan spun everything in my favour. So it was this playful interchange between us that first introduced me to the British public. And Terry, bless his heart, let me get away with it. He was so wonderful to me I didn't have a thing to worry about. I thank him to this day.

'The public loved this witty banter between them and the press instantly picked up on it,' adds Michael. 'Terry would call Mum Honey Gloriford, GBH, even Gus Honeybun after the rabbit on TVS. I think everyone saw her as a dedicated working mum, very much into family. She also came off as being a little bit naive – that was part of her great success. People could really tune into that.'

Once the worry of the handover was behind me, I could concentrate on the hard-core aspects of the popular current events programme. I sat up half the night, reading up on international news and top political figures. For me it was a huge switch from Northern Ireland politics to world issues. One morning I was told I'd be doing an interview on the situation in Lebanon and Don couldn't help but chortle, 'What do you know about the Middle East?'

Back in Northern Ireland I'd always turned down the

list of prepared questions from our research department because I'd been so accustomed to constructing my own interview. This time I knew I was on shaky ground, but fortunately for me John Gurnett, now producer of the Jimmy Young Show, was there as a walking encyclopaedia. I followed my outlines to the letter. 'You sounded so knowledgeable!' they congratulated me afterward with their tongues firmly in their cheeks.

The two weeks standing in flew by. I was enjoying the thrill of working in the Big Smoke in a totally different league. It proved to be two of the most challenging weeks of my life.

On the Friday of my second week David Hatch, head of Radio 2, called me into his office. I imagined we'd have a cup of tea and he'd say, 'You didn't do too badly, you didn't let us down.' It had been a marvellous experience. I was proud of myself. Maybe if I was lucky they'd ask me back sometime to do another stint?

'Look,' said David straight away, 'we're very impressed with the job you've done. How would you like your own programme?'

I was astonished. This wasn't at all what I expected. In fact, they wanted me to start right away, in October. I couldn't wait to get home to tell everyone. I could have skipped across the channel.

No sooner had I broken the news to my exuberant family than I began to worry. I couldn't just up and move to London. My life was in Hillsborough: my family, my roots were there. And my television career. I was established now, prominent and comfortable. I'd got the programme down to a finely honed art. Here I was, the proverbial big fish in the small pond. Did I really want to take the risk of starting all over again in another market?

Not to mention opening myself up to the scrutiny of the merciless British press? Would the discerning English public ever accept a newcomer from Ireland, and a woman at that?

Yet, admittedly, the timing couldn't have been more ideal. Caron and Paul would both be off to England in September to Bristol and Guildford respectively for their schooling. No longer would I see them only at Christmas. Michael was about finished at primary school and he too was in transition. Coincidentally Don had been given a rare, prestigious opportunity to go to South Africa on a three-month directing project beginning in January.

And I'd been doing 'Good Evening, Ulster' for nearly three years. The hugely popular ground-breaker had become a staple for viewers and was certainly on solid ground. If ever there had been a perfect set of circumstances to move on, this was it.

As it turned out, we were all set for a family holiday in Florida so it was a perfect opportunity to make the decision. The decision was unanimous. 'I say go for it, Mum,' Caron was the first to say. 'It's a fabulous opportunity. Take it,' urged Paul. Even Michael, just turning eleven, was excited about the great adventure of moving to London.

But it was naturally my husband's comments which carried the most weight. 'We don't want to hold you back. If you didn't take the job, you'd always look back and say, "What if?" You'd always wonder. I don't want there to be any regrets. It's a marvellous opportunity, once in a lifetime. If you want to do it, we're all behind you.'

We decided that January would be a better time to start – I'd be able to fulfil my UTV contract and we could have Christmas in Ireland. As I told my new London bosses of my decision, I was caught up in a mixture of excitement and terror. It wasn't a lack of confidence in my abilities. My background had prepared me well. I could handle anything from celebrity chat to tough news reportage. I'd done street stories, live broadcasts. I was an experienced presenter. I think it was simply the idea of scale. The audience was larger, the celebs bigger, plus I'd be operating in one of the major media centres of the world. If I failed, the fall would be that much harder.

There was something else as well. Whereas the bosses at Ulster Television recognised the move as a stellar opportunity, the public at large couldn't initially grasp the logic. Their reasoning was, 'Why would she leave a lucrative position in television to go back to radio?' They saw it as a step down. In fact, I even got a bit of flack about it in the *Belfast Telegraph* with a cartoon that read: 'It's Not Funny, Losing Our Honey, Must Be the Money'. That put added pressure on the need to succeed. After all, my contract with the BBC called only for a three-month try-out. If it didn't work out would I come back to a bitter chorus of 'I told you so's?'

Next came the prospect of moving. We left the house in Hillsborough pretty much intact, intending to rent it out if everything worked out in London. I planned to take only a bit of furniture, some favourite crockery, and a few cherished mementos to add a touch of home to my new place.

Come January I bade farewell to family and friends. Mum, although elated for my big opportunity, took my departure the hardest. 'London, why it's a million miles away,' she cried. 'I'll never get to see you again!' Irish mothers never give up their children, no matter what their age. I promised I'd be back soon and often.

Saying goodbye to Don proved even more wrenching than I had expected. There we were, both of us on new adventures. In twenty years of marriage we'd never been separated for more than twelve days and certainly had never been half a world apart.

I decided to go over to London two weeks before I was scheduled to start work and get settled in. The only places I knew in London were Piccadilly Circus, Trafalgar Square and Oxford Street, so I had a lot to learn. Finding a place to live became the first and overwhelming priority. I had endless conflicting advice about living right inside London, or right outside. It was quite by accident I settled in Sevenoaks, Kent. Someone suggested it had an excellent school for Michael, which indeed proved to be true. As luck would have it, right across the street from the school was a house for rent called Courtyard Cottage. I found it to my liking and, more importantly, I could afford it.

I quickly discovered how provincial my world of Northern Ireland had been. My commute to work there, for instance, had taken exactly fourteen and a half minutes. Now I was faced with a two-hour drive every day in and out of a bustling metropolis. I remember taking a dummy run with a map in hand just to make sure I could find my way to the BBC.

We'd been such radio buffs at home from the days of Children's Hour, Workers' Playtime, and the Billy Cotton Bandshow – and here I was standing outside the imposing edifice of Broadcasting House. Do I actually have to open my mouth and say something in there? I remember thinking. I suddenly became self-consciously aware of my accent and its possible negative associations. Would the door shut before I could even step inside? As I nervously settled down in Studio E, where producer Colin Martin had just taught me how to self-operate the control panel, I learned that a TV crew from Northern Ireland had come to film my first day on the job. I wanted to make them proud of me.

The opening record of the first programme was 'On the Opening Night'. I remember deciding to sing along in hopes that the audience would see how relaxed I was. 'I want to be there, on the opening night . . .'

My first guest was Lord Lichfield. I chose Patrick because I considered him something of a good luck charm. I'd had him on my first television show in Ulster and he also later became one of my first guests on 'Sunday Sunday'. Patrick was married to Leonora, daughter of the Duke of Westminster, who had a family seat in Northern Ireland, giving him a bridge between the two countries, well known in Ulster and, of course, a major name in London. I knew I could count on him to spin some good yarns, leaving me free to concentrate on all the new technical equipment I had to cope with.

I also had singer/actress Diana Dors on that first week. My God, I thought, I'm sitting here with this legendary bombshell and getting paid to do it. You can imagine how knocked out I was when she stood in for me on my first holiday from Radio 2.

Another guest on the show that week was Esther Rantzen. She had just had a baby son and been given a hard time in the media for breastfeeding her baby in public at a literary lunch. Despite the fact that she had discreetly gone into an anteroom, the papers jumped on the story with banner headlines. When she came on the programme, infant in tow, Esther requested I not mention the child's presence. However, it was lunchtime and

Esther was breastfeeding. When I opened the microphone the unmistakable sounds of suckling came over the airways. I looked at her and immediately knew I had to say something: 'In case the listeners think Esther's sucking on something or perhaps someone's sucking on Esther, she's breastfeeding her baby at the moment!' Everyone in the studio went into hysterics, including Esther. Another first in the history of radio broadcasting – and a story Esther thrives on to this day.

Everyone in Northern Ireland had been warning me about how cold and unfriendly Londoners would be. On my first morning I was walking down the endless corridors of Broadcasting House when, way in the distance, I spotted this man coming towards me and it seemed to take hours for our paths to cross. Eventually we drew closer and I said 'Good morning,' and he went 'Do I know you?' So I said, 'Not really, I just thought I'd say "good morning".' 'Oh, how jolly nice,' he said. The next time I saw him he greeted me like a long-lost friend. 'Good morning, how are you, how was your first day?' Sometimes you have to make that first move to break that old English reserve.

There were times when it seemed as if female broadcasters did not exist. When Radio 2 moved to a new building, someone forgot that women might want to go to the toilet. There had only been a men's room installed. At first we had a situation where the girls had to go either one floor up or one floor down. Then a few of the announcers got together and decided, 'Look, this is too much hassle. We're not going up or down floors late at night. Let's make this bathroom unisex.'

Actually I found I had the best conversations with my male colleagues in the loo. Steve Wright, the Radio 1 DJ, and I used to meet in there every day before our programmes. We had some terrific chats washing our hands side by side. As I was leaving he bade me a loud farewell, saying, 'Gloria, I'll see you tomorrow in the loo same time, same place.' The look on people's faces as we left I'll never forget. We only had a ladies' room installed late in 1992. I actually miss our old unisex loo.

We lost Maureen Lipman one day as she was due in the studio. Later she came dashing in full of apologies, declaring, 'You do meet such a nice class of people in that unisex loo, don't you?'

Apparently in certain circles the hallowed halls of the BBC were held to be haunted. I had done a Halloween special in Londonderry, Northern Ireland one October. At the end of the programme, I took a call from an engineer and medium who told me I had a spirit hovering nearby (and nothing to do with the whisky). 'I feel it follows you around, particularly in the BBC corridors and in Studio 8.'

What a crank, I scoffed to myself. The following Boxing Day I'd finished a programme in an almost eerily deserted BBC when someone came into the studio. 'I'm just here to do a bit of repair work,' he told me and then stopped short. 'By the way, if you remember, I'm the one who spoke with you at Halloween about the ghost.'

I felt a sudden stab of panic, being alone in this empty, mammoth place with this obviously deranged stranger. 'I don't like to think about it,' I said curtly, trying to avert a conversation.

'Oh, you've no need to be frightened,' he affirmed. 'The spirit I feel is a woman, petite, with grey hair and she hovers over your left shoulder. She's friendly, a guardian, watching over you. She's particularly strong here in this building, walking the halls and in this studio.'

From his further description I had to admit she sounded a lot like my paternal grandmother. Strangely enough, I was no longer afraid. In fact I found the idea comforting that someone in the family might be looking out for me.

Fortunately, it didn't take long at all to settle into my daily routine. Even the two-hour commute became incorporated into my work schedule. I'd use the time to go over interviews, mentally write scripts and listen to tapes. I found this particularly invaluable when dealing with a guest like comedian Barry Humphries. He's very specific as to who he's coming on as on any given day. So I'd have to prepare for three people: the outrageous Dame Edna Everage, the permanently plastered Les Patterson, or, of course, Barry himself.

My daily commutes became indispensable in other ways as well. If I were contributing to an album or performing a number for a charity event, I'd put on the backing track and practise my vocal. It also became my private time for reflection, daydreaming, or simply an escape from the relentless demands of my always hectic work week. It's surprising how two hours can fly by if you learn to use them well.

To try and lessen the load in those early days or in bad weather, I used to take the train on the odd day. Once I missed the train at Charing Cross and had a half-hour wait until the next one. I decided to go into a hamburger place and have a bite to eat while I waited. As I sat there reading the paper a woman asked, 'What are you doing here?'

Totally taken off guard, I replied, 'I'm having a cup of coffee and waiting for the train.'

'But that's completely ridiculous,' she snorted.

'Why do you say that?'

'My dear, you would never see Terry Wogan or Jimmy Young waiting at a station for a train. They all have chauffeurs to take them to and from work!' I was obviously such a disappointment.

Interestingly, many people have a certain image of those in the public eye and get upset if they don't adhere strictly to that mythical standard. They never imagine that you do your own shopping or clean your own toilets.

After I'd been doing Radio Two for a while, the door opened to yet more fabulous and exciting opportunities – a programme with the BBC World Service, a chat programme for London Weekend TV and I even maintained my Ulster connections with a programme for UTV. A singing appearance on the 'Val Doonican Show' led to a big break presenting the six-week summer series, 'Saturday Live From Birmingham'. We had some great names, including John Hurt, several of the 'Dallas' stars and 'Star Trek's' Spock, Leonard Nimoy – displaying his nine pairs of Vulcan ears.

We booked Sylvester Stallone too at the heady heights of his 'Rocky' days. He and his entourage pulled up in six black limousines, but as he got out I was startled to find a much smaller figure than the larger-than-life action hero depicted on screen. Because of the boxing connection we had decided to bring on legendary fighter Henry Cooper. When we brought Henry back to the dressing room to meet Stallone, you could see Sylvester pushing out his chest, nearly popping the buttons on his immaculate hand-stitched silk shirt, trying to stand tall next to this imposing figure. It was all I could do to keep from laughing.

That first year inaugurated a tradition of guests who would make repeated appearances on the show. One was the incorrigible but lovable Les Dawson. In all the years I interviewed him I found nothing that was sacred. Nothing, that was, until the birth in 1992 of his beloved daughter, Charlotte. I'll never forget the pride in his voice as he came on Radio Two, a brand new father in his twilight years. He proudly showed me the photos. One in particular depicted him sitting beside the bed in his pyjamas, nursing the baby. I couldn't resist saying, 'Les, you look as though you've just given birth.' 'I have to tell you, Gloria,' he quipped gleefully, 'I don't even have any stitches!' Les was there that day to plug the second volume of his autobiography, *Tears of a Clown*. Appropriately, the final line reads: 'The clown will cry no more.' Since his death I'm sure his wife Tracey has gained much consolation from the fact that she and the baby brought him so much happiness and love.

Another guest I've got to know quite well over the years is latin crooner Julio Iglesias. His first appearance in 1982 was memorable; his English was so appalling we actually had to prerecord and then edit the interview so that he could be understood. However, with each successive yearly visit, his command of the language has grown impressively, to the point where it is now virtually flawless. 'I can have a lot of fun in English now,' he often tells me, his eyes twinkling.

In 1983, Julio's popularity in England exploded to the point that he arrived at the studio with an entourage of fourteen. He was clad in a magnificent full-length mink coat, cutting a stunning figure with his white teeth sparkling out of a handsome, tanned face. As he entered the studio, he slipped off the mink and let it drop to the floor in a grand gesture. None of his people made a single attempt to retrieve it. Finally after a few awkward moments Julio himself picked it up off the floor. I caught his eye and we both exploded with laughter.

Three years ago he came on the programme and as we idly chatted in between records he happened to ask, 'What are you doing over Christmas?'

'We're going to Los Angeles and then plan to spend New Year in Vegas.'

His eyes lit up. 'It just so happens I'm in Vegas over New Year. You must come and see me. Listen, I'll give you the number of my assistant. Call her and she will set everything up.'

'You'll regret that,' I said, 'there are eight of us in the party.'

Sure enough, all was arranged. It turned out that Julio was singing at an exclusive private party for the 'High Rollers' at Caesar's Palace. Once the cabaret was over Julio told us, 'I'm having a party up in my suite. Please, you must come.'

We found our way to the executive floor, heavily guarded expecting hundreds of people to be there. It turned out there were only fourteen specially invited guests at this posh shindig. We all had a wonderful conversation with Julio and then he told us he had to leave for his next concert. 'Stay as long as you like,' he told me. 'There's plenty of food and drink. Feel free to use the suite all night.' With that he flew off for Miami in his private jet, leaving us to party the night away.

In October of my first year in London I got a call from director and choreographer Norman Maen. 'How would you like to be on the Royal Variety Show?' he asked. The

Royal Variety! To think of all the years I had watched it from my armchair in Northern Ireland, and now he was actually asking me to be part of it. I was stunned and it took all of two seconds to say 'yes'.

There is something about the Royal Variety that turns everyone into a gibbering wreck, even big international stars. However, by the night of the show I was only hoping to get through the performance without making a fool of myself in front of the Queen. I was teamed up with Esther Rantzen and newsreader Jan Leeming in 'Anything You Can Do, I Can Do Better' from *Annie Get Your Gun*. We'd barely had adequate rehearsal time due to our conflicting schedules. And we had rehearsed everywhere, almost down to the broom cupboard. Just when I felt we had the number down to a passable performance, we arrived at the Theatre Royal in Drury Lane to a major shock: the stage was enormous compared to the poky places in which we'd rehearsed.

'What are we going to do?' the three of us cried to Norman Maen. 'How are we ever going to adapt all the moves to the large stage with no time?'

This was a very complex dance number with intricate choreography. As fate would have it, who should be on the bill with us but Howard Keel, who'd of course made the song famous in the now classic movie version. In desperation I took hold of Howard backstage and pleaded, 'C'mon, you've got to coach us here. How do we do it?' Howard managed to calm us all down and lend much desperately needed moral support. As it happened, it launched the beginning of a very special friendship that has blossomed over the many years since.

The curtain went up and suddenly there we were, the three of us in our specially designed swede cowgirl gear with short, fringed skirts, boots, hat and trusty holsters ready to take our marks. We started with our backs to the audience and one by one would whirl around to identify ourselves. In fact, the only way we made it through was via Norman's instructions from the wings, yelling 'Turn! Turn! Turn!' We were elated at the mere fact that we all three ended the number at the same time. Howard rushed up to congratulate us. 'Good going, girls! Well done.' Later on, that snippet of television history made it into the annals of 'Television Hell'.

I don't believe anyone could have had a more memorable, magical year than my first in London. Just when I thought it couldn't possibly get any better, there came the highlight, by way of complete surprise. I was doing the show as usual one early afternoon in January 1983. My guest was one of the stars of 'Coronation Street', Stan Stennett. We were having a great time, fielding calls from listeners eager to learn more about their favourite soap star. In the middle of all this my producer suddenly said, 'Take a mystery caller.' Puzzled, I peered at him through the glass, but nonetheless took the phone call. 'Hi! This is Eamonn Andrews.'

I was immediately blown away. Eamonn Andrews actually listens to my show, I beamed. Why, this is brilliant! 'Hello, Eamonn. Tell me, what brings you on the line today?'

'I just wanted to ask Stan how he felt last week when he was hit with "This is Your Life".'

I was so busy preening myself over Eamonn's interest in the show that I didn't immediately catch sight of a camera crew and Andrews himself walking towards me from opposite sides of the studio. When I saw the familiar red book in Eamonn's hand I still didn't get it. It never occurred to me for a split second that I could be up for the honour. It wasn't even in the realm of possibility. After all, I'd only been in London a year.

Then Eamonn popped out with the proverbial line, 'Gloria Hunniford, this is your life!'

My face fell 'as long as a Lurgan spade' as the Irish put it. I was in utter shock and still thought it was some kind of joke. All I could think of was, do I play a record now? Somehow I got going on the news, then Eamonn said, 'We've got a broadcast van waiting downstairs. Let's go.'

It was arranged for someone to take over the records, but as I was hustled downstairs and into the van, I realised the news was almost over and it hit me that I had still another half hour to fill on the programme. My head was swirling; I absolutely could not think. Just for something to say I started to give a running geographical commentary as we began our journey. 'Now we're heading down Mortimer Street and I can see people poking their heads out of shops, waving and smiling. Cabbies are pulling up alongside the van smiling, "Good on you Glo! Congratulations!" My God, this is all so overwhelming and unbelievable.'

I looked out the back window and couldn't believe what I was seeing. Crowds had gathered, spilling on to the streets. A few people were actually running behind the van. I felt as if I was part of a spectacular parade. In that exhilarating moment came the realisation that I had been accepted by the British public. It was truly one of the warmest, proudest and most privileged moments of my life. The only way I got the broadcast completed was by interviewing Eamonn about the various catches he'd made on the show over the years.

As we pulled up outside the Theatre I began to appreciate the magnitude of planning that went into these shows and found myself wondering how they managed to pull this off without eliciting even a shred of suspicion from me.

The night before had found me working at London Weekend Television. Caron was at home babysitting Michael. I rang them at quarter past five to check in and told them I would ring back when I had finished and was ready to leave. 'Oh, we'll probably be in bed,' said Caron. 'We're going to turn in early tonight.' With that, the two of them left Sevenoaks, dashed up to London, had dinner with the family and the crew, and went through a rehearsal. By the time I came home, they were tucked up asleep in bed.

'All the family had been put up in the White House Hotel and the get-together we had the night before the programme was fabulous,' recalls Paul. 'it was quite ironic the way we managed to pull it off without Mum being any the wiser because she was a bit miffed about missing out on our reunion.'

The following morning Caron was supposed to come into work with me and she had to think of a thousand ways to stall. 'I'll take the next train up, Mum. You better get going.' Apparently there was a car tucked away behind the pub up the street, containing people connected with the programme armed with walkie talkies and charting my every move. As soon as they saw 'the suspect' leave the house, they packed Michael, who had hidden in the pub on his way to school, into the car, along with Caron, who had packed a change of clothes for me to wear on the programme, and sped up to London for the show.

The entire 'This is Your Life' presentation was laced with wonderful touches and astounding surprises all along the way. The whole family was assembled, including Mum, who was clearly glorying in the proceedings. The figures from my past read like a delightful who's who: my first vocal coach, Gail Sheridan, friends and schoolmates from Portadown, like Mary Peters and Anne Thompson and her daughter Christine, scores of fellow performers from the 'Tiny Tots Review', some a little balding, but I recognised every one. Greer Walker, their leader, was there. I was told that the streets of Portadown were all but shut down the night the programme was aired. Everyone was at home watching the show!

They'd flown over my great friend from Old Fort Henry in Canada, Henry Knotek, and Gerry Kelly and Dan Gilbert from my broadcasting days in Northern Ireland, as well as contemporaries Terry Wogan, Jimmy Young, Jan Leeming, Esther Rantzen and Val Doonican.

'And now, Gloria,' announced Eamonn, 'we're going to Hollywood for our next guest.'

Wait a minute, I thought in confusion. I don't even know anyone in Hollywood. Live via satellite from the set of the television mega hit 'Dallas' came the voice of my new friend Howard Keel, who went on to give a warm, touching tribute.

Caron recalls the event as one of our proudest family moments. 'It was truly one of the highlights in Mum's career. I remember calling up all my friends and telling some of them, "You've got to watch television tonight; we're all going to be on!" Until that show my friends at university didn't really know who Gloria Hunniford was. Being on "This is Your Life" is a sign that you've really arrived.'

To this day I still play the tape of that occasion every now and again. Michael was only eleven at the time and it's very endearing to hear how he sounded at that age. It has been a particular comfort after my mother's passing away that I have been able to watch her in this most special of circumstances, happy, proud, surrounded by her family, something of a celebrity herself that day, a wonderful sparkle in her eye. I remember how Mum dined off that appearance for months and was even invited to speak to the Mothers' Union in Portadown about it. May Hunniford was a star!

9

Sunday Sunday

I'd only been in London a matter of days when I was called to the office of Greg Dyke, now the managing director of London Weekend TV, then the new producer of the Six O'Clock Show, presented by Michael Aspel and Janet Street Porter.

David Bell, then head of London Weekend, had taken notice and got in touch with me.

'We've got this chat show lined up and we think you'd be perfect. The hour-long format would include interviews with visiting performers plus a critical element.'

Already I was getting excited. 'What time is it slotted for?'

'Sunday afternoon at five o'clock.'

Instantly I was deflated. I'd been fortunate throughout my career in broadcasting during peak hours, either mornings or evenings. Who on earth would be watching at that hour in the afternoon?

In fact, it turned out to be a brilliant slot. It was perfectly sandwiched between the lunch and dinner hour and provided entertainment for those rainy, gloomy Sundays from October on when everyone was stuck inside with nothing to do and not much on television. Even though it was London .based and not networked nationally, the city was a mecca for entertainers, so we had no problems getting top names booked for the programme.

'Sunday, Sunday' debuted in September 1982 and proceeded to run to spectacular ratings for an impressive nine years due to the best back up production team. When I look back on the log I've kept of guests, I realise there's hardly a film, Broadway play, or blockbuster novel that I didn't cover during that period. On the most personal level, it was the ultimate fan's dream come true. Imagine the thrill of meeting my childhood cinema idols Charlton Heston, June Allyson, Kirk Douglas, Audrey Hepburn, Leslie Caron and, of course, Jimmy Stewart.

The first time he came to the programme, Jimmy said, 'I'll always remember your name, because my wife is Gloria.' A favourite recollection of his was about acceptance. His father ran a hardware store in the American Midwest and, being from the old school, was totally against his son becoming 'one of those playboy movie actors'. Even after Jimmy was a huge name in Hollywood he could hardly get his dad to acknowledge his career. The senior Stewart had no interest, to the point of never even seeing his son's films. Finally in 1940 when Jimmy won the Academy Award for Best Actor for his role in *The Philadelphia Story* he returned to the hardware store to find a surprise waiting for him. 'I finally knew my dad accepted me,' he smiled, 'when I saw my Oscar displayed on the bacon slicer.'

Personalities ran the gamut from the long-winded Stewart Granger, whom I had to all but throttle to get in a word edgewise; to the tight-lipped Robert Mitchum, he of the cowboy 'yups and nopes'. We always had a planning meeting every Tuesday to find out who would be on the programme. On this occasion, Charles Brand, the producer, said he had good news and bad news. 'The good news is we have Robert Mitchum, the bad news is he's the worst interviewee in the world.' Robert is an interviewer's nightmare, providing the terror of the deadly silent gap. I thought it would be different with me, but it wasn't. After a few minutes I realised that. When he gave one of his classic one-word responses, instead of leaping in and trying desperately to fill the air with another question, I didn't say anything. He then felt he had to back it up with a proper answer. An effective ploy for a very awkward situation.

Part of my job is making a difficult interview look effortless. But no matter how much research you do you can't do much about someone who's feeling a bit off colour or doesn't feel like talking or has a case of the nerves. Lee Marvin, that cinematic tough guy, came on the programme absolutely petrified because he hadn't done any interviews in eight years. Barbara Knox, who plays Rita Fairclough in 'Coronation Street', was similarly anxious as she'd never done a chat show. I told her, 'Don't worry. I'll keep the questions coming.' A talk show host sometimes has to play confessor, amateur psychologist and general hand-holder.

There are times when it is easy to lose all concentration and just go blank. Once Jeff Goldblum was a guest.

He has huge staring eyes and can really psyche you out. I had all my notes on my knee but found myself totally mesmerised, to the point that I couldn't tear my eyes away to glance down at them. I interviewed him recently about *Jurassic Park* and the stare is still the same, but the more I get to know him the more it seems like fun, flirty eyes rather than anything sinister.

Another guest who had the same effect was Egyptian actor Omar Sharif. As I was interviewing him I kept remembering those velvety liquid brown eyes staring out of the screen in *Dr Zhivago*.

Comedians have always found the *Sunday* set a place to shine. I remember Frank Carson, known for never being short of a word or two, coming on with the quip: 'What's a poor man's jacuzzi? A fart in the bathtub.' The audience howled with laughter. I managed to ask him one question – after that I couldn't get a word in edgewise. I tried everything – sitting on his lap, putting my hand over his mouth, but nothing can stop Frank on full throttle.

Freddie Starr is the undisputed king of unpredictability. I never know what I'm in for when he comes to the programme. Once he ate the flower display of daffodils I had next to me. Another time he made a grand entrance by crashing right through the set. Freddie has honed a marvellous Elvis Presley imitation and decided to show it off on the programme. While in the middle of his gyrations, he managed to catch my eye. 'No, please don't come over here,' I cringed. Of course he did and performed these outrageous bumps and grinds right in my face. He gets a kick out of those blushes.

Now and then a guest not particularly known for humour ends up being hysterically funny because of a terrible blunder. David Frost comes to mind because I did my 'Hello, good afternoon and welcome' to David Frost,' and he made his entrance in ebullient style, bursting on to the rostrum and bringing everything crashing down, including a bookcase filled with glassware, plants and knick-knacks. The poor man was kicking away flowerpots and pop cans while the tape rolled. But he vowed to try and get me stronger sets.

There was an unfortunate accident in 1989 with singer Billie Jo Spears, whom Terry Wogan calls The Singing Harpoon. When she arrived on the set she bent down to kiss me and the ash fell off the end of her cigarette, burning a mammoth hole right through my skirt. She was thoroughly, visibly embarrassed and apologised profusely. Following the interview, she got as far as the door then rushed back up to the studio. As I stood there she plucked off her wonderful gold earrings and handed them to me. 'I really want you to have these,' she insisted. 'I can't replace the skirt and you must have some sort of compensation.' Since then it's become a running gag and the last time she was with me on Radio 2 she arrived with skirt in hand.

I've often found it's the serious actor who can spin the most wildly entertaining and funny stories. I never imagined the current toast of the Shakespearian stage, Kenneth Branagh, would tell a tale that would have the audience rolling with laughter, but that is exactly what happened when he related an incident that happened one night during a performance of *King Henry V* at Stratford-Upon-Avon.

He had lost a pair of gloves pivotal to the scene. 'I got to the end of the battle and discovered the gloves had fallen out of my belt. It's tricky in Shakespeare trying to improvise, but I started making things up. I looked around with glazed eyes, walking amidst all these dead bodies, trying to look moved by the battle scene, all the while trying to catch someone's eye in the wings, desperately whispering ''Where are the gloves?'' Finally someone came to the rescue. ''Ah, Fluellen, I'm glad thou art here because I have some gloves which I would like for thee to get me, please. Go away now to get them and bring them backest.''

'This guy came back with what looked to be a pair of motorcycle gloves. In the meantime, I'd found the gloves I'd dropped, so while he came back in triumphant, shouting, ''Hark, I've found the gloves!'' I had to counter with ''I'm glad thou hast found the gloves, but I have foundest yet another pair!''

For some strange reason I reduced movie tough guy Rod Steiger to tears. When he first came on the Brooklyn-born actor cried while discussing his daughter, who is a great opera singer. Later in the interview he burst into tears when he talked about his breakdown. Strangely, it all started with a humorous sequence when I asked him about some of the 'bombs' he had made over the years. 'I have done some dreadful pictures,' he bellowed, 'some dogs. Like *The Unholy Wife*, with Diana Dors. I did a thing called *The Kindred*, where slime eats people alive. I think now they're going to be exhibited in a museum of oblivion somewhere.'

But then the conversation took an abrupt turn when he disclosed he took on some of those abysmal flops to fight through a harrowing long-term depression. 'For two years I didn't do anything. I'd come down in the morning, sit on the couch and tell my wife good morning. The next thing I said was good night. That was it. I just sat there, unable to move. Finally my agent called me and said,

"Listen, they don't know if you've retired or whether you're dead or alive. You better do something." And as an actor and a human being I panicked. That scared me to death. That got through the cold jell that surrounds you mentally and physically when you're in that state.' He broke down into tears and confessed, 'I knew I had to do something and I did. But it was tough. I'm not ashamed. I was fighting to just do something to show them I was still alive.'

Towards the end of that conversation Rod spoke about the unfailing support he got from his new young wife. As it turned out, his depression was caused by a chemical imbalance, and when this was discovered, he was helped tremendously by medication. At the worst point, however, he seriously considered suicide. Of course, talking about this brought the tears welling up again. Rod said he never went through with the suicide because he worried, of all things, about bleeding all over the floor and his wife having to clean up the mess.

We've been fortunate in landing several exclusive interviews on Sunday, Sunday. For example George Harrison, who rarely speaks to the media. George was enjoying phenomenal success at the time with the all-star band, The Travelling Wilburys.

He revealed how the group was formed purely by accident. 'I was asked to record an extra track for an album I was making. I was having dinner with Jeff Lynn and Roy Orbison and they said, "If you're going to do it tomorrow we'd like to come along." The only place we could find to record at a moment's notice was Bob Dylan's garage. Tom Petty was there so I thought, why not get them all to sing?' They ended up doing an additional ten tracks and The Wilburys were born.

My lasting memory of this superstar was, after the interview, saying tentatively 'Was it all right?' I couldn't help thinking back to seeing the Beatles in Belfast in the early Sixties. I certainly didn't 'hear' them but in the midst of the mayhem I thought of my friend at UTV, Mike Kent, who in 1961 before they hit the big time turned the Beatles down for a fee of five pounds, saying 'I wouldn't take this rubbish for nothing.' He has dined out on that story ever since.

George also revealed that the late Orbison was far from the dark, melancholy figure his songs depicted, but in fact had quite a sense of humour. 'He was a complete "Monty Python" fan. He knew the words to all the songs, including "Sit on my face and tell me how you love me". He would get a giggle going and by the end of it we'd all be in hysterics. He was a really sweet and lovely guy.'

People imagine when you are doing a chat programme, that all the guests have dinner beforehand to get to know one another. Personally I don't like to talk too much to the interviewees before the programme apart from saying hello and the usual pleasantries. I always imagine if they tell you part of the story of their interview, they think they've already told you the story and don't come up with the goods on the night. So I prefer to keep it fresh. The big names are usually rushing off afterwards – so apart from a drink in hospitality that's it.

However one particular night the guests on 'Sunday Sunday' were Britt Ekland and Slim Jim, Sharon Maughan – the Gold Blend coffee girl – cricketer David Gower and some of the Coronation Street cast. For some strange reason they all decided they wanted to go out for dinner after the show so we booked a table at the legendary Joe Allen's in Covent Garden. A huge table was set up for us just as you entered the restaurant so all the names were the focus of attention. I remember clearly my brother Charles, his wife Libby and children Michael and Kerry were visiting London and joined us for the evening. They sat at one end of the table watching all these famous names chatting away and loving the fact that every well known person entering the restaurant came across to where we were to 'work the table'. For example Michael Ball when he was at No. 2 in the charts, Michael Crawford when he was in *Phantom of the Opera* and the ubiquitous Chris Biggins. As we left my brother said 'Is every studio night like this?' Little did he know that normally it was the cafe up the road.

Sometimes the most entertaining stories happen behind the scenes. On one occasion we had one of the handsome hunks from the 'Dallas' series who will remain nameless for obvious reasons. This tall, good-looking charmer commanded the attention of the girls backstage and in the offices. One lucky researcher I'll call 'Gail' was given the enviable job of taking him to tea at Claridge's, to do the research interview. 'When we walked in everybody stared at us. It felt really good, you know – maybe they thought I was his lady,' she related proudly.

He gave me a scintillating interview, then, after we had come off air at nine-thirty, we went up to hospitality. Normally the guest stay about an hour, but at midnight he was still there, surrounded by a dozen women, including producers and secretaries.

The following week I came into the studio and asked, 'How long did our "Dallas" friend stay?'

The place erupted in laughter. Someone said, 'Ask Gail.'

She proceeded to tell me a marvellous story about her

experience. Part of the researcher's job is to see a guest off the premises. If someone stays until one o'clock the researcher has to stay. Apparently this dishy actor was about to enjoy his Thanksgiving meal at the hotel and, not wishing to eat alone, invited Gail along. 'I had the most fabulous time,' she recalled, 'eating a turkey dinner with loads of champagne.'

At one point, her host suggested, 'Why don't you come up to the room and freshen up?'

'So we went to his room,' said Gail, 'and had a bit of a snog. I didn't get home until about five in the morning.'

That's one hell of a long time to freshen up, I thought to myself.

Anyway, Gail, who had a live-in boyfriend, did the soft key in the door bit and crept up the stairs in hopes of not disturbing him. However, as soon as she reached the bedroom he bolted up in bed bellowing, 'Where the hell have you been?'

'This guy from "Dallas" was my interviewee and I had to go to dinner with him and . . .' she stammered.

'Don't give me that shit! Nobody from some bigtime show is gonna take you out to dinner. So tell me where the hell you've been all night!'

The episode caused her boyfriend not to speak to Gail for three solid weeks. Another two weeks passed and suddenly a call came from America. It was none other than the 'Dallas' stud on the line for Gail. It finally dawned on the boyfriend that she'd been telling the truth. He was so taken with the fact that this mega TV actor wanted to date his girl that he proposed marriage – and that was the last we saw of a very good researcher.

With all the huge names that have appeared on 'Sunday Sunday' it was rare for the crew to get excited over any guest. That is, until the day Bette Davis walked on set. At this point she was very ill with cancer and the interview was among the last she would give. But illness did not for a moment diminish her status as the long-reigning queen of Hollywood. Detailed instructions were given to me by her young assistant and her appearance was stage-managed to the last detail. When she made her entrance I was told I had to walk forward and put my hand out, not to touch her, but just in case she wanted to lean on my hand as she came down the step. Then I was to walk over to the set and let her sit down first.

By her side everything was meticulously arranged exactly to her order. There was her book placed so the title was in view. Next was a black patent-leather handbag open with a lace handkerchief just out over the top. In front of that was placed her silver goblet from which she always drank her own water. Then there was her silver ashtray and her famous cigarette holder. I was told not to touch anything.

You could hear a pin drop. All these usually blasé technical people were simply in awe of her, this indomitable screen legend. Despite the fact that she was obviously very frail, she still maintained her star aura. Those 'Bette Davis eyes' could still command your attention.

Although that interview went down as the high point of 'Sunday Sunday', my personal highlight had to be the opportunity to chat with Audrey Hepburn. She represented the romance of my youth, the wispy dancer turned actress whom every girl wanted to emulate. An all-time favourite film is *Breakfast at Tiffany's*, which I enjoy time after time. I longed to be the waif-like Holly Go-Lightly, brazenly whistling on the street outside Tiffany's.

Something of that impressionable schoolgirl was still with me when Audrey came on the set. Incredibly she still looked the same, lean and elegant with that swan-like neck and sweet elfin face. We spoke about the passion that consumed her life, no longer films, but her work with Unicef. She spoke too, about her relationship with long-time companion Robert Wolders, a fellow Dutchman, and how she could never complete her mission without his support.

I subsequently interviewed Audrey in Switzerland when she had just returned from a trip to famine-engulfed Somalia. She spoke movingly about how she had seen mass starvation in other parts of the globe, but none as devastating as this.

She was due to appear in the 1992 Royal Variety Show and I was so looking forward to seeing her. At that point it was known she'd been ill, but no one realised just how seriously. When she died so unexpectedly early in 1993 I was greatly saddened. For me and so many of her fans who identified with her whimsical, endearing, courageous characters it was a great loss.

I recalled how we had once spoken about the scarcity of film roles for a woman her age. 'I receive scripts that have me playing someone younger, which is ridiculous,' she said, 'or those that have me playing someone older, which is equally ridiculous. I just want to play myself.' Ironically, Audrey's final role was in Steven Spielberg's wistful and nostalgic *Always*, where she portrayed an angel. How very fitting.

Her place at the Royal Variety was taken by Leslie Caron and you can imagine how thrilled I was to discover I was sharing a dressing room with her, Rita Rudner, the American comedienne, and singer Kiki Dee. On royal occasions such as these it's always a squash – the girls all in together in a fairly small dressing room. Apart from introducing the royal variety I was also there to do my Radio 2 from rehearsal day. I didn't mean to gibber but very quickly I heard myself telling about seeing *Gigi* on my way to Canada when I was seventeen, how I had loved the film so much that I had called my daughter Caron after her and how I would let Caron stay up at night to watch her movies. She took it all in her stride, and gave me a very good interview for Radio 2. When you spend a long time in a confined area rushing around, getting dressed, sharing nerves, you all feel like bosom buddies after a couple of days. We all got through our respective bits on the show and as we headed off to the grand party afterwards at the Dorchester I realised when I was packing my things away that Leslie Caron was looking a bit like a waif. As if she had read my mind she said 'Do you think I could possibly come with you?' In a flash, life for me had gone a circle from all the pleasure she had given me as a seventeen-year-old to now when I could do her a favour. My son Michael helped her pack up, carried her bags to the car and our driver Brian took care of her for the rest of the evening. She was so grateful and I was just thrilled.

Sunday Sunday went by the board in the ITV franchise re-shuffle, but I'm quite philosophical about these things. I had nine years of the top names providing endless memories. After all, where else could a small town girl from Ulster get to dance with Andy Williams, stand toe to belt-buckle with John Cleese, sing with Cliff Richard and flirt with Gene Hackman?

Whoever said 'Never on a Sunday?'

10

Pulling Up Anchor

I don't remember Mum ever being sick. She was the constant, indestructible hub of our family, holding us all together. I only ever saw her cry a few times, when her own mother died and, when Dad passed away. Even in later years, although she had a few gynaecological problems, in the main she was still as healthy as ever.

In January of 1987 I had just stepped off the plane from a relaxing, refreshing holiday in the Seychelles when I received an urgent message at the airport to call Caron.

Her voice sounded strange and faraway. 'It's Nanny, Mum. She's had some bad news. She found a lump in her breast. The doctor's run a biopsy. She's going to have to have the breast removed.'

I dumped my bags and took the first plane over to Belfast. I'd no sooner arrived at the hospital when Mum was wheeled out of surgery – I'd arrived on the day of her operation. My sister Lena sat with me, filling me in on the details. It had all happened so quickly, I felt as though the world were spinning out of control. All I could think of was that I'd been off having a splendid time for myself while my mother was facing the greatest trial of her life.

Following the surgery Mum was absolutely distraught over losing a breast. She'd always been such a proud woman, so fastidious about her appearance. Now she was inconsolable and I was suddenly sick with fear and uncertainty. The doctors were confident that they had removed all the cancer, but could give no guarantees it wouldn't spread.

It should never have reached this drastic point. Some eight months earlier Mum had gone to a doctor about an irritation on her breast. Simple eczema was the diagnosis and a medicated cream had been prescribed. My mother came from that generation which never questioned its doctor. His word was law and if he said it was eczema it was eczema. She kept thinking the medication would clear up the problem.

Tragically, the next time she brought up the condition, it was far too late. Her nipple was inverted, a clear sign that a malignancy had developed. All those precious months wasted, when the cancer might have been contained. I couldn't suppress my anger at the GP in question. 'I cannot believe that this woman came to you all those months ago and you gave her a tube of cream. For God's sake, it was right there on her sheet and you never asked her whether the irritation had cleared up even though she was here to consult you about different medical problems! What do you have to say to my mother now? She lost a breast because of your negligence. She trusted you with her life.'

I returned to London and following one of the most despondent and discouraging weeks of my life, I went back to the hospital at the weekend. Heading down the corridor to Mum's room I couldn't believe what I saw. There was my mother, all her IV drips packed in a smart Marks and Spencer's bag, walking gaily down the hall. 'I just told them I'm off to do my shopping!' she said. The twinkle in her eye was back, she had the old spring in her step. It was the most glorious sight I could wish for.

Her resilience absolutely amazed the entire family. That she could bounce back so quickly gave us all renewed hope. Pulling out her specialised brassiere, she'd crack, 'I'm putting in my falsies now. Here, feel this, Gloria. Just like the real thing, eh? Looks good as new, don't you think?'

Having confounded us all with her quick recovery Mum returned home to her life in Portadown. My only disappointment was at her refusal to journey across the channel to visit me in London, which I could nevertheless understand. Her illness had made her insecure in that regard. 'I really don't want to travel any more,' she told me. 'I just want to stay near home in case I get ill again.'

Several months later, on my birthday on 10 April, Neagle (my other half at the time) and I were heading out for a quiet dinner when I had a call from a couple of friends, Debbie and David Noble, who own a hotel in Sevenoaks. They asked us to join them for a drink en route. We were having a pleasant chat at the bar when I happened to glance over to a corner of the room where a large party had gathered. I did a double take and realised, I know some of those people! Upon further scrutiny I discovered they were all familiar faces, every one. What a fabulous birthday surprise!

Then slowly, the crowd began to part to unveil a figure seated at the very heart. It was Mum, smiling and buoyant, wishing me a happy birthday. Mum, here in London!

Caron had sprung the whole thing. She'd gone to Portadown and brought Nanny back with her and collected all the family and best friends. My mother was able to stay a glorious week with us. It was the best and most caring gift I could have had.

I could hardly bear to let Mum go. Maybe it was because I sensed an air of finality about the visit. In fact, not long afterwards I got a call from Lena. 'Mum's broken her arm,' she told me. 'She was getting on a bus and as she grabbed on to the handle to pull herself up the bone just snapped.'

I thought it odd that a break should occur in this way. I wondered if maybe Mum had a bone problem like osteoporosis. But after she was admitted to the hospital, we had another devastating setback. Doctors discovered that the cancer had spread to the lymph glands.

I knew what this meant. It had only been a matter of months since her mastectomy, and for the growth to have spread so far so fast meant she was losing ground quickly. But we were determined to keep Mum's spirits up. My sister Lena was the greatest support during those difficult times. She was specially close to Mum, lived near her and saw her every day. My frustration was being on the other side of the water, but in a way it helped Mum to look forward to the next visit. I remember coming into her hospital room one day armed with a lacy nightgown. I did her make-up and hair and put on an elegant pair of pearl earrings. She looked sensational. Mum was still an uncommonly beautiful woman with extrarodinarily fine porcelain skin.

She was in phenomenal spirits that day and for a time felt remarkably well. Once again, she had emerged with that typical pluck that astounded all of us. She was in

Left: First photo of Caron as a baby, she at about 2 months, me at 6 stone 10 oz

Below: Me, Paul, Caron and Don in our first home, the bungalow at Marnabrae Park, Lisburn

Right: Mother and child competition, August 1965, Butlins Holiday Camp at Mosney, Co Dublin. We took first place, winning £100 – Caron reckons she's still owed £50

Left: Brotherly and sisterly love: Caron and Paul

Right: My favourite shot of newborn Michael and me

Below: Michael's christening: Don, Mum, me, Dad and Professor Billy Thompson who was not only godfather but delivered Michael

Below: Happy memories of Marnabrae: Caron aged 9, Paul aged 7 and baby Michael

Left: Raising money for Children In Need: Sonny and Cher, alias grandad Terry Wogan and me with 5lbs of eyelashes

Below: The Val Doonican Show – first major network singing appearance in 1982

Above: Rock and rolling with Cliff

Right: Don, Michael, me and Paul at a recent family wedding

Above: Treasured photo taken shortly before Mum died, 1988

Above: At my 50th birthday: Elsie, invaluable dog-sitter, niece Pamela, Lena and my best friend from Northern Ireland, Anne Thompson

Happy snap with Caron in the *Blue Peter* garden

(Below) Me, brother Charles and sister Lena in Sevenoaks – the Hunniford kids

The rebel rousers at Radio 2: Tel, Ed Stewart, Jimmy Young, John Dunn, Sarah Kennedy, Derek Jameson, me, Ken Bruce and Ellen Jameson

A Radio 2 birthday: Ken Bruce, John Sacks, me, Brian Hayes and Ed Stewart outside Broadcasting House

Top: Proud day: Caron's wedding in June 1991 – best man Peter Powell, Russ Lindsey, Cathy Comerford and my great nieces Linzi Cinnamond and Francesca Fowler

Above: Another proud day: Michael's graduation from Bristol University. Me, Caron, Michael and Don

Left: Happy days at Christmas in St Paul de Vence: Caron, Paul, me and Michael

such good form that one day she decided, 'I want to go home.'

I was a bit more cautious. 'I'm not sure, Mum. Why don't you give it a trial weekend and see how you manage.'

'Oh, nonsense. I'm fine. I'm perfectly well enough to get on by myself in my own home.'

We moved her bed downstairs to the sitting room and installed a stylish commode. Lena would look in on her as well as a neighbour.

Her broken arm still hadn't healed and had left her incapacitated. Inevitably there were times when she was left alone. One day she had an accident. She was rolling out of bed when she fell on her bad arm. She must have been lying helplessly on the floor for at least half an hour until a neighbour, Jack, found her and had to lift her back into bed.

That incident marked a disheartening turning point in Mum's illness. She was terribly upset, totally beside herself that Jack had seen her in her nightie, that he had to help lift her on to the toilet. To watch my mother lose her dignity was almost more than I could bear. On top of that, I saw the realisation in Mum's face that she would never be able to manage on her own again. I knew at that moment we were losing the battle. She slowly began to go downhill.

Mum was the last person on my mind before I went to bed and the first when I got up in the morning. It was like an ongoing nightmare. There were times I was at the studio on the phone with the doctors, often sobbing, and minutes later had to go on air and transform myself into a sunny, lighthearted radio presenter. It's known as the red light syndrome, believing you have a responsibility to the audience to leave your troubles off the airways. Listeners have enough problems of their own. They don't deserve to be burdened with yours. But in a way the daily programme was a marvellous way of diverting the mind, if only for a few hours.

Towards the end of June, the ravages of the cancer began to take their inevitable toll. Sometimes Mum was caught up in hallucinations, ranting and raving. Most of the time, however, she was quite lucid, for which I was grateful. Even as I watched the increasing signs of deterioration and her obvious suffering, I never reached the point where I could say, it would be better if she died. I would have done anything to keep her in that bed. Just to talk to her, hold her hand, know she was there. It was incredibly selfish, I know, but I couldn't let her go.

I'd just got back to Sevenoaks from a heartbreaking weekend with Mum when I got the news. She had gone into a coma and it didn't look good. I raced back to the airport, thought the hour flight would never pass, and when I eventually reached her little ward it was empty – I hadn't made it back in time. Like all the family, I was devastated, but in a strange way I took consolation in that I had been the last one to feed her her last meal of jelly and ice cream before she slipped into a coma. That Monday, 6 July, 1987 she passed away. In Ireland we have open coffins and in a curious way I was comforted by the fact that Mum was near me, looking so beautiful, almost radiant, her face a countenance of peace. I used to sit for hours just looking at her. In a childish way I felt I was keeping her company until the casket had to be closed for the funeral processesion to Seagoe Cemetery, then everything inside me suddenly went to pieces. Mum was really gone. How could I ever accept it? How could I bear to never hear that laughter, never to see the light in her eyes, never to hear her call my name? As absurd as it sounds I felt like a child who had been orphaned. There was this grown, successful woman, a mother of three, all of forty-seven years old, feeling utterly abandoned and hopelessly adrift.

Losing my father had been bad enough. I remember how I thought I would never get over it. But losing the second parent was far worse. You think your parents are always going to be there, that they'll live forever. Suddenly I was no longer huddled in their safe shadow. There was no one standing between me and my own mortality. I wanted to run back to those idyllic days of innocence when Mum and Dad always had the answers, when they could fix everything.

Clearing out the house, going through Mum's belongings was a chore Lena and I could barely cope with – a situation I'm sure many people can identify with. We had to do it in stages, as the flood of old memories became intolerable. Coming across the scrapbooks Mum had kept brought forth an avalanche of tears. She'd first begun keeping clippings of my father during his career as a magician and then began a scrapbook of my own childhood performances. She started one again for me as an adult and then kept one for Caron. Eventually she even had to start a scrapbook for herself – she'd become a bit of a celebrity in her own right with her high-profile visits to London for television appearances and interviews for magazine articles. The last photo taken of the two of us together was a cover shot for *Chat* magazine, featuring May Hunniford's homemade bread recipes.

There was one moment that was particularly bittersweet. We came upon an unopened box of chocolates stored in one of Mum's pride of places. On Mother's Day

Mum had been guest of honour on the 'Des O'Connor Show', along with the mothers of Michael Parkinson and Russell Harty. They were put up in a posh hotel, had a limousine at their disposal and of course, that night did the show.

Michael, Russell and myself weren't allowed anywhere near the studio – it was the mothers' night. The following day I took Mum out for tea at the Ritz, which was a thrill for her. As soon as we sat down, the head waiter, Michael (who's been there some forty years, but was originally from Ireland), came over to our table and said to Mum, 'Madam, I thought you were simply wonderful on the "Des O'Connor Show" last night.' She beamed and revelled in the attention. Then as we finished our tea Micheal returned, bearing a huge silver tray with an oval box of fine Ritz chocolates, exquisitely packaged, finished off with a large lace bow. He presented the gift to my mother saying, 'Madam, just because you were so wonderful on television last night I wonder if you would accept this on behalf of the management.'

As Lena and I drew out that box, still unopened, we realised how much Mum had treasured that gift as a memento of one of the highlights of her life. I'm sure Michael had no idea how this small but thoughtful gesture meant so much.

That first Mother's Day following her passing was especially trying. On the radio show that day I had to read out people's letters as part of our Mother's Day competition. I found myself really choked over it and several times had to cut swiftly to music. However, when I look back, I am thankful that there was nothing left unsaid between Mum and me. We'd been a demonstrative family, always the hugs and kisses goodnight, always the 'I love you's'. I feel so sad for those who've left loved ones behind with regrets and 'if only's'.

When the time came to sell the house it was like severing the final tie. Our whole lives were in that cozy two-storey terrace – it had been the only house our parents had ever lived in their entire married lives. Lena and I wandered through one last time, each of us lost in our own thoughts. I could still hear the echoes of laughter as we chased Charles up and down the stairs; I could smell the delicious aroma of Mum's wheaten bread drifting out from the big range; I could see all of us gathered round the kitchen table swapping stories that we've since passed on to our own children.

Backing out of the doorway that final time was like pulling up anchor in a deep harbour. Even though Lena still lives nearby with her family, I felt strangely rootless. I still go back for weddings and funerals, to see old friends and family, and to work. But it's no longer quite the same. I haven't been back to see my old home. I can't seem to bring myself to drive down the road. I think it's something I will never get over.

11

Disaster and Redemption

Mum was always fond of saying, 'Bad things happen in threes.' Whether it was just circumstances or indeed my mother's heartfelt superstition coming to pass, I'll always remember 1989 as the year my life took a very downward spiral.

I've been very fortunate that throughout my career I've come away relatively unscathed from the tiny percentage of hate mail, crank calls and threats that are, sadly, an occupational hazard of public life. If the front office screened out these unsavoury communications I never knew about it.

One unnerving episode, however, did occur during my first year at Radio Two. As an Irish woman broadcasting in London I was not so naive as to believe my presence wouldn't stir up strong sentiments in certain circles. As it happened I was on air that tragic day of 20 July 1982, when bombs exploded in two related terrorist incidents. In Regent's Park a bomb went off beneath a grandstand as the Royal Green Jackets were giving a concert. Simultaneously an explosive set in a car boot discharged in Hyde Park as a troop of the Queen's Household Cavalry was riding by to take part in the changing of the guard at Whitehall. Nine soldiers were killed and fifty wounded that day. Eight horses were also dead or so badly injured they had to be destroyed.

The disastrous news was being filtered in during my programme and needless to say it was a difficult, emotionally wrenching broadcast. When I came off air I saw the staff milling anxiously about, including my BBC bosses, all wearing serious expressions. 'There's been a threat on your life from an anonymous caller,' I was quickly informed. Apparently an agitated listener, upset over the day's turbulent events, had phoned up in a fury. 'Look at all this devastation in London. Get that Irish person off the radio or I bloody will! She'll be killed if she leaves the building.' I wasn't about to play hero and stick around. The top brass took it seriously enough that I was forced to leave the building by a secret exit every day for some time afterwards.

As a public figure, of course, you're almost certain occasionally to encounter people who overstep the bounds of acceptable behaviour. I remember one man who, come rain, hail, or snow, waited outside Broadcasting House for me every single day for five years. Unlike the usual stalwarts, who were merely starstruck fans waiting for an autograph or an off-the-cuff photo opportunity, this fellow seemed intent upon making me a major part of his life. One day he hurried up to me with an exuberant greeting and bent to kiss me. I immediately placed my hands on his chest and pushed him away. I told him firmly, 'Don't ever do that again!' Fortunately, he seemed to get the message and the incident was never repeated.

That kind of episode was rare until the spring of 1989 when I began receiving disconcerting letters every day from a sixty-five-year-old man. A typical note would read: 'You know you're the only one for me. I'm going to be at the George Hotel at 4:00 and I expect you to be there.' When I didn't show, his follow-up missive would generally express a bit of intimidation: 'I sat there for four hours and you never turned up. How dare you do that to me?'

Next he bombarded me with flowers and gifts and somehow managed to get hold of my work phone number. When he told me he had booked us aboard a worldwide cruise on the *Queen Elizabeth II* for Christmas, complete with accommodation in five-star luxury hotels, I realised this was now clearly a potentially dangerous obsession.

It started to get really scary, though, when he began to lurk in the foyer of Broadcasting House. Then he crashed the ultimate barrier. He started taking the train to Sevenoaks, found out locally where I lived and showed up at my front gate. Frankly, I was surprised at both his appearance and demeanour. Expecting some menacing psychotic, instead I found a balding, rather meek older man, more sad than intimidating. I told him politely to go away and he did, hanging his head as he silently plodded back down the road towards town.

But he kept coming back. One afternoon Michael was at home studying for his A levels and tried to ease the situation with a bit of psychology. 'Look, why are you doing this? Don't you have any family? Do they know you're doing this? You know Mum doesn't want you here, she doesn't want to see you. So please go away now.' Still, however, he wouldn't leave. Michael, growing more perturbed, now turned to a different tack. 'This is useless, what you're doing, it's just a figment of your imagination. It can't lead anywhere, don't you see that? It will never amount to anything. I want you to leave right now!' When he still refused to budge, an exasperated Michael filled a bucket of cold water and tossed it over the poor man, leaving him soaking wet and utterly dejected.

Finally, that May I had no other choice but to seek an injunction against this unlikely stalker. He was ordered to remain at least one hundred and fifty yards from my workplace and five hundred from my home. In addition, he was not to write letters, make phone calls or express any behaviour that could be interpreted as harassment.

Time and again, however, he breached the order. The police were brought in, but they could do little more than talk to him and escort him away. Ultimately I was forced to take him to court. I didn't want to see this man behind bars, as clearly this was not the place for him, but I felt compelled to do something. At the hearing it was brought out that he had been charged some five years earlier with sending a hoax letter bomb to Margaret Thatcher. I believe Princess Margaret and the Director General of the BBC have also been bombarded by his letters. He was also undergoing medical treatment for other related behavioural problems. Thankfully, the High Court made him answerable to the judge. This time, if he broke the injunction he'd be given a stiff jail sentence.

In fact, he did breach the order and continued to come up to the house, but by then I had installed a top-flight security system with electronic gates and twenty-four hour video surveillance. We simply ordered him to leave and he did. Eventually, the visits stopped altogether.

After that, for a time, we became alarmed by anything even remotely suspicious. One morning at the BBC I received a call from Elsie, who looks after my dogs. 'The bell went off at the front gate,' she told me. 'And this strange-looking man said he had a package, so I walked down and asked who it was from. He said he didn't know.' Elsie then spotted a second man in the car, which seemed suspicious as there were never two drivers sent out to deliver a package. She added that they were speaking in 'some foreign language'. Naturally, this left me very uneasy. Elsie gingerly took the large, heavy parcel and, not knowing what to do, rang up a friend of mine, who instructed her to place it in the garage. I notified the police, all the while worrying about a friend's Rolls Royce we were keeping in the garage. I had visions of a bomb exploding and the pricey car being blown to bits, not to mention damage to the house.

The local police arrived and cautiously entered the garage. As they approached the package we all held our breath. Carefully unwrapping layer after layer of paper, the contents were duly exposed. It was a complimentary selection of previous books by my co-author Geoffrey Giuliano! Poor Elsie kept apologising over and over as we all had a good laugh.

I had just come home from a skiing holiday in 1989, feeling especially fit and healthy. This particular Sunday evening I called on my pals, Pam and Div Harris, to join Neagle and me for a game of doubles tennis followed by a roast dinner and an evening's chat. We decided to utilise the indoor courts at Michael's school in Sevenoaks, a top-rate facility covered by a felt-like surface.

I could never really give Neagle a proper game but he was always a sport about it, recognising it was good practice for me. On this particular April day I felt a plucky sense of wellbeing from my recent adventures on the slopes. Ironically, that would prove my downfall. The competition was hotting up when Div lightly popped the ball just over the net. I had to make a split-second decision whether I should make a run for the ball or not, knowing Neagle would reach it easily. But by now, my adrenalin was pumping. Here was the chance to really show my stuff.

Time was suddenly stopped in a sequence of freeze-frames. The ball was skimming towards me, just within my reach, then I was running forward on the offensive. My toe caught on the surface and I did one of those staggering runs out of control, not falling down but not able to recover my balance. Eventually I went crashing into the metal post that supports the net, with my shoulder taking the full brunt of the impact.

I heard my bones snap, the force of it rattling inside my head, sizzling through my entire body. I became aware that I was tangled in the net, my neck twisted horribly. Above me were the ashen faces of my friends staring down in terror, certain that I'd broken my neck.

I managed to get on to my back and that's when the shock set in. It was as if I was outside my body, looking on as an observer. I wasn't crying, at least not consciously, yet water was pouring from my eyes. Though I wasn't aware of it, my arm was grotesquely twisted out of position, as if someone had yanked it off and then stuck it on backwards.

The ambulance arrived and by now the pain had set in, a tortuous agony unlike anything I'd ever experienced before. When the attendants tried to help me on to a stretcher I couldn't bear to let them as much as touch me. Somehow I was able to crawl on to my knees so that the medics could slip an oval rubber ring around my arm and inflate it to give support. Only then was I able to bring myself to a standing position and begin the excruciating walk to the ambulance. Just as I gingerly made my way into the vehicle I saw Neagle faint and collapse to the pavement. The ambulance men didn't know which of us to concentrate on.

I was rushed to a local hospital, knowing I'd broken my arm, but totally unaware of just how badly. Following literally dozens of x-rays, the doctor finally came out. From the grim look on his face I knew it was something quite devastating. 'Look, he said, 'I don't know exactly how you've done this, but you've mutilated your arm and shoulder. It was broken in fifteen places.' The ball and socket of my shoulder had completely shattered and the humerus was broken as well, which accounted for the arm hanging backwards.

He regarded me curiously and said, 'Listen, if you were an ordinary housewife, all I could do for you would be to put your arm in a sling and send you home. You'd be lucky to have forty per cent movement of your arm.'

I fought back a rising panic and indignation. This so-called compassionate doctor had the nerve to suggest one course of medicine for the celebrated and another for 'ordinary' people? It went against everything my parents had raised me to believe.

'But in your case I would advise you to try and get it operated on.'

'Well fine,' I said impatiently. 'Let's do it.'

'The trouble is, Ms Hunniford, shoulders are known

as the forgotten joint. There are very few people who operate exclusively on shoulders. It's very tricky because the shoulder controls all of your back and arm muscles right down to your fingertips.'

'Just tell me who to go to then.'

He gave me a blank stare and replied, 'I don't know. I really don't know.'

In all fairness to this fellow, he had only recently begun practising in England. But by now I was exasperated, furious and terrified. I'd been lucky all my life healthwise. I'd never even been in a hospital except for the delivery of my children. Now I was faced with the real possibility of losing over half the movement in my shoulder. This was all magnified by a wall of pain that was by now nearly unbearable. So, with my arm wrapped in a sling and numbed by painkillers, I went home.

For some strange reason I insisted that my guests stay for dinner. Looking back I couldn't have been in my right mind. But there I was, still in shock, doped up on pills, incapacitated and practically strong-arming Pam, Div and Neagle into eating my roast. I had it in my head that nothing serious was wrong and that I must carry on, business as usual. I refused to let this thing conquer me.

Well into the night, exhausted and in total agony, I was running on sheer determination. There had to be someone who could help me. Settled uncomfortably on the settee with my old address book from Northern Ireland I decided to conduct a little journalistic research on orthopaedic specialists. Ironically, the one positive spin-off from the two decades of violence in my home country was the unparalleled expertise of the Ulster surgeons. As I had conducted interviews with many of these gentlemen back in Belfast, I retained several private numbers and now, thankfully, had them at my fingertips.

At last I made contact with a doctor in Hollywood, County Down. 'I vaguely remember seeing an article in the *British Medical Journal* about shoulders,' he told me. 'It seems there are only a couple of people in the country who actually do them, so let me get back to you.' He rang me back a couple of agonising hours later and supplied two names. Both were available – one said he could see me Wednesday, the other the next day. How I was to bless finding Mr Ian Bayley, one of the best orthopaedic surgeons in the country.

The next morning couldn't come soon enough. I spent the worst night of my life, siting upright in an armchair, getting little sleep, unbearably groggy from my medication. I couldn't lie down as it was impossible to put my weight at all on my right shoulder.

The next day I discovered just how disabled the accident had left me. I couldn't put on tights, nor a blouse or even tie my own shoelaces. I had to jimmy myself into a pair of trousers and then threw enough over me to cover myself and get to the orthopaedic hospital in Stanmore.

Following an examination and a thorough study of the x-rays, the doctor regarded me gravely. 'The question is not will I operate, but can I. I'm afraid it's very badly mangled.' After further scrutiny of the x-rays he came back and said, 'Well, I believe we can do something for you after all. Let's say we give it a go. I'll operate tomorrow morning.'

My initial elation was quickly tempered by my overwhelming anxiety. It was just beginning to sink in how serious it was, if even the top orthopaedic surgeon in the British Isles was hesitant to try and piece me back together. This was a mighty big gamble. As if my emotional state weren't fragile enough, the story was somehow leaked to the press. The operation was to take place in the Clementine Churchill Hospital in Harrow on the Hill, and in a weird way I was really looking forward to it, anything that would help the situation. I remember looking at myself in the green operating gown and thinking how dreadful I looked with my hair pulled under my cap. As I came out of the bathroom I bumped into a girl in a tweed topcoat, and I said 'Who are you?'

It turned out she was a reporter from one of the newspapers, ferreting out the big scoop. Somehow she had managed to slip into a private ward and private room. Here I was at my most vulnerable. I was livid, at breaking point. I let out a scream. 'Get out of here!' I immediately got on the phone and rang up my press office. 'You call that paper and tell the editor to get this woman out of my room,'' I yelled. It was all too much.

The operation took three-and-a-half hours of refined and delicate work. The ball of my shoulder had exploded into pieces of bone splayed in all directions. The surgeon collected all the fragments and pulled them together in a mesh of wire, stapling them with dozens of metal clips. In addition, two giant steel pins were placed from shoulder to elbow. Afterwards the doctor told me, 'There's no problem with the humerus mending. That's elementary. The big question now is the shoulder. How it heals will determine the amount of movement you'll have.'

Discharged from the hospital after a week, I lay low, totally zonked from the anaesthetic and the shock to my system. Despite this, I was determined to start back to work the following Monday. It was the old Irish ethic once again, rearing its stubborn head.

But even my determination couldn't overcome the seriousness of what I'd been through. My arm was swollen right down to the fingertips, with little or no movement. Despite all the metal I was downright scared of doing anything which would pull it apart again and I had to give in to another week off. It was only then I realised that day to day life was not going to be that easy. A good night's sleep was out of the question. I couldn't bear to lie on my side and had to resort to an oversized angled pillow for support.

Getting dressed, of course, was another adventure. With my right arm and hand totally out of action I felt as useless as an infant. It took me ages to manoeuvre into a pair of tights. I could not fasten a brassiere and still can't to this day, so I had to wear an all-in-one teddy. Applying make-up was an exercise in hilarious futility. I'd kneel before the mirror, anchor my face on the bureau and just about manage to dab some colour into my cheeks. I couldn't even run a comb through my hair. It got to be a running joke that everyone who came to the house was required to perform that particular chore. Michael, of all people, got to be quite proficient at backcombing.

The sheer kindness of people overwhelmed me. Letters, gifts and flowers all poured in. I'll never be able to repay my gratitude. A dear friend, Beryl Marks, made a nine-mile drive every day to make meals for the entire family that could be zapped into the microwave. Beryl was simply a godsend. She'd wash my hair, put it into rollers or tong it, anything I wanted.

Shopping and simply anything I needed during the day was done by Rod Thropp and Paul Welsh, who have an antique shop in Brasted village, about four miles away from where I live, and to this day are an important part of our family life.

I eventually returned to work, managing to get through the first few weeks in a daze. I was crazy to push myself so hard, but I was determined not to let my arm disrupt my life too much. Just two weeks after the accident I was back in action at the BBC. I had to be moved to a special basement studio with my angled pillow to prop me up plus a bottle of painkillers and herbal tea at my side. The BBC was kind enough to send a car for me each day. My shoulder was so sensitive I had to request a vehicle with an automatic transmission – I couldn't even endure the thrust and shudder of manual shifting.

I was due to begin a new national television quiz show 'That's Showbusiness'. Kenny Everett was captain of one team and I was to be the other. Jo Gurnett, agent to us both, had a serious chat with me about whether I'd be able to meet the contract. She pointed out 'If you miss the first you'll have to skip the series but you'll have to think very seriously about your health.' We had a chat with the producer John Kaye Cooper who said 'I'd rather have you doing it with a broken arm than not at all.' So we decided to go ahead with those weekend trips to Manchester to record the thirteen-week series. That angled pillow was to become my constant companion on and off the plane. I really had to be more or less put to bed at nights so Jo booked a suite with an inter-connecting door in case I needed anything during the night. It became impossible for her to go every weekend so she said, 'There's only one thing for it, Kenny Everett will have to take my place.' It struck me as hilarious that Ev, normally associated on television with Sid Snot and Cupid Stunt, was playing nursemaid. What a story that would have made, Gloria and Ev sharing a hotel suite – all of course 'in the best possible taste.'

A few months later a follow-up x-ray revealed that two of the pins had somehow snapped inside me. I was crushed at this setback. In August I had to undergo yet another operation when the doctor reopened the shoulder and hammered in two stronger pins.

Ironically, at the same time I was contracted to host a BBC fitness programme called 'Go For It'. This involved a slate of thirteen shows, all to be filmed in one week. The producers wanted me to go ahead, despite having my arm in a sling. My designer, Allison Ritchie, however, came to me with an idea. 'Why don't I create a few designer slings for you?' It was ingenious. Before long I had one to go with every outfit, not only colour coordinated – pink, purple, polka dots – but all featuring exotic materials and elegant edgings. Allison came up with a frilling around the collar that was very flattering, especially in tight shots. Incredibly, this exploded into somewhat of a phenomenon. Photos began popping up in the papers, highlighted by my appearance at Wimbledon wearing a black hat with matching black sling with lace edging. The public reaction was so overwhelming I considered putting out a line of designer slings. A man even came up to me and quipped 'That's the nearest thing to socially acceptable bondage I've ever seen!'

Then came another blow. The ball and socket was healing beautifully, but inexplicably the humerus was not. There was still a gap between the two halves of the bone and the tissue was soft. The doctor brought up the possibility of having to do a bone graft. That would mean taking some bone marrow from my hip and grafting it on to the humerus. The prospect of yet another operation that would leave me with a second debilitated limb and lay me off for a minimum of six to eight weeks left me completely demoralised.

On one of the x-rays, however, the doctor detected a

tiny bit of mending. Quickly seizing on any glimmer of hope I asked, 'Would it make any difference if we wait another six months and see if there's more improvement?' Thankfully he said it wouldn't. I had been given a reprieve.

This is where Kenny Everett comes in again. He was something of a regular on Sunday and I was looking forward to seeing him. At this point I was out of my sling but still carefully nursing my arm. I introduced Ev and in typical fashion he charged on to the stage bellowing, 'Oh darling, darling, how wonderful to see you!' In his exuberance Kenny went to grab me and do a tango thrust over his knee, but instead he came at me too fast and knocked me backwards. I went crashing to the floor and the blunt metal edge of the step caught me smack across the shoulder blades. I cried out, 'Oh, my shoulder, my shoulder!'

The audience burst out laughing, thinking it was all part of the act. But when they saw me lying on the stage, my face etched in pain, there came a gasp of nervous tension and then a clipped silence. I lay there, panic rolling through my head. After all I'd been through, two operations, so many months of healing, was I now back to square one?

I was carried off the set. Beyond all this, something within me roared up, a kind of absurd 'the show must go on' mentality I could never seem to shake. 'Look,' I said to the crew, 'if I don't go on again right now, I'm never going to get through it.'

I made myself get back out there and, operating on some kind of autopilot, made it through to the end of the show. Immediately afterwards I was taken to the nurse's surgery, where I burst into tears. The initial examination indicated a possibility that I might have cracked my spine. Poor Kenny. He stood there awkwardly, profusely apologising, feeling terrible. But I was so preoccupied I couldn't consider his feelings. He, above everyone else, knew what I'd been through.

Thankfully, follow-up x-rays confirmed no further damage. Meanwhile Kenny did everything to make up for his gaffe, sending me flowers and cards. 'In future, maybe I should just write to you!' he quipped over the phone one day. I know he felt terrible about it all and, after all, he didn't do it on purpose.

If I were to regain any significant movement in my shoulder I had to undergo a rigorous programme of physiotherapy. A lovely German woman named Helga put me through a severe work-out. I called her my 'physio-terrorist'. When the pins broke, one of the tabloids blamed it on too intense a therapy programme, which was totally untrue. I felt so bad for Helga because she had done so much to help me.

The uncertainty of my prognosis weighed heavily on my mind for nearly two years until at last I got the definitive news I had been praying for. The humerus had healed completely. I wouldn't need the bone graft after all. It was one of the happiest days of my life. I now have eighty per cent movement in my shoulder.

The injury, of course, has changed my pace. I used to run everywhere, up and down stairs, along the corridors of the studio – but no more. Now I walk everywhere and step very gingerly. Sad to say, I will not venture down the slopes any more. As a skier I fell a lot anyway. But I have returned to tennis, something I thought I'd never do again.

It was Cliff Richard and his manager Bill Latham who

were to encourage me to play again. For a few years now Cliff has had a very successful pro-celebrity charity tournament at Christmas. Last year he changed the venue to the indoor arena in Birmingham and around July he asked me if I would consider playing in the tournament. I pointed out that I had never been 'that good' and was very dubious about the future capability of my shoulder but I agreed to turn up to support the charity, if only to start off a game or draw a ballot ticket. He even arranged a few practice games at Wimbledon which was beyond my wildest expectations. Just to turn out there was a real treat. Sue Mappin, former tennis champ, and her assistant Mary, who run Cliff's tennis trail to find young players, were our doubles partners. Sue was wonderful at helping me get over my worry of using the arm again for tennis. She taught me to serve all over again, bearing in mind I don't have full rotation. Within a few months I was ready to show up at the tournament and Cliff had promised to partner me on the day. What he didn't tell me was that there would be eight thousand people watching. What a baptism of fire! Also taking part that day was Virginia Wade whom I had watched endlessly on television back in Northern Ireland. As we were about to take on Virginia and Frank Bruno, I thought, hang about, here is Virginia Wade ready to serve to me and I'm supposed to hit it back. Undoubtedly the star that day was four-year-old Jack who is one of the promising youngsters on Cliff's trail. At one stage when I missed a crucial point heading towards the semi-finals a wisecracker from the audience shouted 'Cliff, swap Gloria for Jack!' I also recall I said 'yours, Cliff!' a lot but the climax of the story is that on my sideboard I have a wonderful cut glass vase to commemorate getting through to the finals.

Thinking back on it now, the tennis accident proves that out of every negative situation there is a learning process, and what it has given me is a small and humbling insight into physical disability. I now have a greater admiration for those who have had to overcome endless disabilities to continue with their day to day life. All I have left is an unflattering eight-inch scar across my shoulder but that's only vanity and in the long term not important at all.

Towards the end of that trying year I was especially looking forward to Christmas. The holidays had always been family time and 1989, if a year of trial for me, had been terrific for the kids. Caron had become engaged to her manager, Russ Lindsay; Paul had started up his extremely successful sound company; Michael had passed his A levels and gone on to university. We had a lot to celebrate. Surely, I thought, the worst was behind me.

On the evening of 10 December we held a dinner at Hever Castle in the verdant Kent countryside for the entire family and several close friends. I had invited everyone over to the house for pre-dinner drinks and catch-up chat. I was in a mellow mood, reflective and content. The house was so warm and cozy with touches of red and green trimming the furnishings, the tree exquisitely decorated, its fairy lights sparkling, casting a delicate, magical pattern on the ceiling. Everyone in the world that I loved was gathered there, all smiling, well and happy.

During our celebration at the castle I noticed Caron was a bit restless. She had acquired a new puppy and had brought it to Sevenoaks for the first time, but she had been hesitant to leave the pup with my own burly canines.

'What if something happened to him?' she fretted.

'Oh nonsense. He'll be perfectly fine,' said Michael, brushing it aside.

'No, I'm sure something's wrong,' she insisted. 'I know the dog's going to be hurt tonight. Something's going to happen to him.'

Come on Caron,' said Russ. 'Don't you think you're getting a bit carried away?'

But my determined daughter insisted on leaving early to check on the tiny pooch. She asked Michael for the key to the house, but caught up in conversation, he was momentarily distracted. Next she asked me for the key. 'Oh Caron, it's in my bag out in the cloakroom, but I'm leaving soon anyway.'

A few minutes later she asked me again. This time I got up and as I made my way across the room I inevitably stopped for a chat with one of our guests.

'Mum,' Caron pressed a third time. 'The key.'

Still I got waylaid and by this time an exasperated Caron had left for Sevenoaks with Russ and Michael.

As we wheeled into the driveway I knew all wasn't well. The front door was open and as I got out of the car I realised the hall was thick with black smoke. Caron, Russ and Michael were bravely heaving buckets of water everywhere. We were all confused and panicked, not believing this was the same house we left a few hours earlier. You can never understand how frightening a fire can be be until you are in the middle of one.

The fire brigade pulled up straight away and managed to contain the damage to the hallway. They figured the cause as faulty electrical wiring in the Christmas tree lights. 'It was like a time bomb,' the fire chief later told me. 'The brass railing at the bottom of the stairs was totally bent with the heat. Had you opened your front door, I'm afraid there'd have been a blast of oxygen causing an explosion which would have likely killed anyone in the way.'

Something which would certainly have happened if they'd had the key. The key Michael hadn't given Caron. The key I hadn't given her. She later told me how they'd pulled up at the house to the sound of the fire alarm and the dogs' frantic barking. The only way to get inside was to break the glass in the back door with a broom handle. The key had been left in the back door, which is something I rarely did. By another twist of fate, the door from the dining room into the hall, which is normally locked, was on this occasion left open, so the kids were able to get through to start fighting the blaze. It was as if 'somebody' had given us a few extra chances. I can't help wondering if it wasn't more than coincidence that all of Caron's attempts to get the key back at the castle had been forestalled. Thank God for my daughters sixth sense. Thank God we were all safe.

The whole of the house was thoroughly blackened from wall to ceiling. Like fools we stayed in the house that night, inhaling smoke into our lungs. I went to bed a blonde. The next morning I awoke with jet black hair.

Virtually everything had to be replaced: carpets, curtains, closets full of designer clothing. It took a team of seven industrial cleaners an entire week to reclaim the house, working from top to bottom. Even this was not completely effective. But as the fire brigade said, I was lucky to have a house to clean at all. Recently I pulled out something from a cupboard and my hand was covered in soot – a full three years later! But material things can always be replaced. I have my family, which is all that matters. It could have been far, far worse.

During that tumultuous year, there were moments when I gave in to self-pity. But it's a valuable lesson in life as to what takes over and helps you through dark days. You only have to look at Roy Castle, one of the most inspirational individuals I have ever encountered. He's long been fighting a valiant battle with lung cancer, this ardent non-smoker who acquired the disease second-hand from a lifetime of late-night shows in smoky clubs. Roy and I did a concert tour of sport/entertainment shows together and so I got to know him quite well. He radiates a positive attitude in the face of this dreaded killer that touches everyone around him. He came on my show just to thank everyone for their support and good wishes. He told how he was given a mere five per cent chance to beat the disease and then said something I'll never forget: 'Someone has to be in that five per cent and it may as well be me.' He's single-handedly been responsible for instilling immeasurable hope to other cancer victims, encouraging them to hang in there and fight on.

I remember him coming to dinner after his chemotherapy treatment had been completed. I later discovered from his wife Alison this was their first social night out since the treatment began. Cliff Richard and his manager Bill Latham were also there. It was the first time we'd all seen Roy since he lost all his hair. What would we say in those first few seconds after he arrived? Bill Latham had the perfect answer. Indicating his own bald pate, Bill said, 'Don't you think Roy and I would make a great pair of bookends?' adding ruefully, 'at least Roy knows his will grow back.'

Sometimes the most memorable interviews come from the public, not celebrity guests. In Northern Ireland, at a time when people never talked openly about cancer, I got a call from a girl who said she listened to the programme every day and wondered if she could join me one day to warn women not to ignore a lump in the breast as she had done. By this stage hers had spread to the spine and liver. She caused a sensation not only in Northern Ireland, but through an interview we did together for 'Woman's Hour' in London. They had heard about this outspoken woman who had a message and apparently hers was the first interview they had had from someone actually prepared to spell out about having cancer.

We became good friends and I used to visit her when she became bedridden. Her only remaining goal at that stage was to hang on until her daughter got married. I'm glad to say she did, but died a few weeks later.

Whenever I ponder grace in the face of adversity, however, one of Hollywood's biggest names comes instantly to mind. I first met Sammy Davis Jr through the musical composer, Leslie Bricusse, who wrote shows like 'Stop the World, I Want to Get Off' and 'Doctor Doolittle', and had written some sixty songs for Sammy. In one of our many conversations Sammy told me of his longstanding desire to play the Albert Hall. I made initial inquiries and decided to discuss it further with him on a forthcoming trip to Las Vegas.

During that trip Sammy arranged for the family to visit him in his private suite at the MGM Hotel. The head of his security detail was Brian Dellow, who hailed from Bangor in Northern Ireland, part of the 'Irish Murphia' as we natives sometimes laughingly call ourselves.

We were met by Sammy's road manager, an elderly, memorable character. 'Hi, I'm Murphy and I'm adorable,' he cheekily greeted us. He then led us through security to Sammy's opulent penthouse suite. There in the middle of this posh room stood an enormous table overflowing with pots and pans, and the wonderful smells of home-cooked food wafted towards us. Sammy loved to prepare his own meals. In another corner sat an immense black leather trunk with shelving that was absolutely stuffed with movie videos. Sammy was an incurable film buff. In addition, there was a Pac Man computer system installed. This, apparently, was how Sammy spent the long, hot days in the Nevada desert.

As we sat in the bar I told him of our plan to try to book the Albert Hall – though I'd never even thought of becoming a promoter I'd managed to arrange the financial backing – and he was terribly enthusiastic. 'If you can set it up, hey, I'm there,' he promised. Unfortunately those plans had to be scrapped when the news came through that Sammy had signed on to do the 'Ultimate Event', that wildly successful road tour with Liza Minelli and Frank Sinatra. It was only afterwards I realised how totally naive we had been in even contemplating it against the 'big boys'.

I'd seen Sammy perform many times. On this particular opening night in Las Vegas he spoke to the audience about his forthcoming operation for a hip replacement, confessing his fear of undergoing surgery and wondering whether he'd be able to dance as well afterwards. I was struck then at the vulnerability of the man, a slight figure propped on that chair centre stage. Yet as soon as the orchestra revved up it was all power and energy, making this pocket dynamo seem invincible.

Backstage after the show, Michael was really impressed with the monstrous limo waiting patiently for the beloved superstar and mesmerised by Sammy who, even on opening night, took the time to chat at length with my son, then fifteen. Everything about the man was first class.

I did one of the final interviews in Britain with Sammy before his untimely death in Los Angeles from throat cancer a few years back. As fate would have it, this segment was particularly memorable, one that I'm sure he looked back on with fondness in his final days. We set up the basement studio in the bowels of the BBC and brought Sammy down for what he anticipated would be a regular one-to-one conversation. He hadn't done any interviews at all in recent times. The astonished, delighted look on Sammy's face said it all as I proceeded to bring out a string of his closest friends: Leslie Bricusse, Lionel Blair, whom Sammy adored because they'd danced together in London, and finally Liza Minelli. Liza recalled the parties of her childhood when 'Uncle Sammy was always around the house. As young as three or four I remember sitting on his lap, telling him all my problems, or when Mum had parties I would sit on the landing looking through the ballustrade railings, gazing down at all the glamorous people laughing, swapping stories and singing, and many times Uncle Sammy would come and join me on the staircase. There was nothing we didn't share.' Not only did this group swap fond reminiscences, but they had a wonderful jam session at the piano we had set up. This, for me, was a rare opportunity to sit back and settle into my original role as a fan. Sadly, it was to be the final time I'd see him perform.

Shortly after Sammy's death I received a call from

Liza. She was performing a tribute to her dear friend at the Albert Hall and asked me for a copy of the tape of that special show. 'I want to get Sammy's laugh,' she told me, 'so I can have it reverberating through the hall during the performance.' What a poignant touch to what unfolded as a moving evening of music and memories.

During those final months of Sammy's illness, I talked with Leslie Bricusse, who kept close tabs on him. I learned that before undergoing throat surgery Sammy opted not to have his vocal cords removed. The operation would have bought him more time, and possibly even his life, but ever the proud, consummate entertainer, he chose to leave his voice intact, willing to risk the odds as he'd done throughout his high-impact, eventful life. Small in stature, yet a giant of a man in his talent and generosity.

Leslie's favourite recollection of the early years of their friendship was of a dinner at the small two-bed-roomed flat in Stanmore, Middlesex, where he and Evie lived at the time. Sammy was appearing at the Palladium, but on his day off was playing at a golf charity do. The Bricusses invited him for dinner afterwards and, expecting two or three people to turn up, Evie prepared a sumptuous meal of duck à l'orange. In due course Sammy turned up – with about twenty-five people in tow. In the end Leslie and Evie were frantically ringing round all their friends for anything they could contribute to the dinner. It was like the feeding of the five thousand.

I got to know Leslie Bricusse through interviewing him. I always loved his stories about how in every musical or film score he writes he composes a song especially for his wife Evie, such as 'My Kind of Girl,' recorded by Frank Sinatra and Matt Munro, among others, 'Someone Nice

Like You' from *Stop the World* and 'When I Look In Your Eyes' from *Doctor Doolittle*.

Hooked on the romantic side, I got him to explain how a friend of his, Vilma Anne Leslie, had introduced them, believing them to be the perfect match. As Leslie said, 'She was right and this year we celebrate our thirtieth anniversary'. He said it would have been lovely to invite Vilma to their celebration party but they'd lost touch years and years ago. Before the end of the programme Vilma had called Radio 2 and the three were reunited. This quirky coincidence was the beginning of a delightful relationship between our families. Leslie and Evie have a beautiful house high up in the hills overlooking my favourite part of the world – St Paul de Vence in the South of France. These days it is a millionaires' paradise with property way beyond the reach of most people. Leslie bought a long time before it became a fashionable spot for the rich and famous. His was the third house in the middle of this upmarket development back in 1970.

It is here Liza Minelli got to work out songs and routines, with Michael Feinstein at the piano. Julie Andrews, for whom Leslie wrote *Victor Victoria*, is a frequent visitor. But stay a few days at the house and it's a question of guess who *came* for dinner. Joan Collins, Roger Moore, Sean Connery. . . . it ends up like a scene from a movie until Roger indulges in his risqué jokes. Through Leslie I also got to know and value my friendship with Gillian Lynne, the former ballerina turned choreographer who travels the world directing and checking productions of 'Cats' and 'Phantom of the Opera'. Gillian and her actor/singer husband, Peter Land, have also invested in property in St Paul – about three houses along the road from the one we rent every Christmas there along with John and Michelle Carlton-Smith and family.

St Paul is a medieval village perched high above the valley which sweeps right down to the Cote d'Azur. Smells and sounds of the valley are quite special and the soft pinkish light is almost beyond description. No wonder all the famous painters went there – Picasso, Matisse, Chagall. One of the most famous restaurants in the world is La Columbe d'Or where the painters traded in pictures for their food.

La Columbe d'Or's culinary skills had nothing on mine when I was staying with Gillian and Peter for a weekend. As we shopped at the market in Vence for one of her special dinners, I heard myself say, much to my surprise, 'I'll do the starter.' My speciality is a scallop dish so I duly bought my ingredients and when everyone went to bed for a siesta in the afternoon, I thought I'd pounce on my opportunity not to be observed in the kitchen. I had the scallops, mushrooms, onions at the ready to be cooked, then opened the fridge to take out the butter. Gilly being a health fanatic I knew wouldn't approve – however, decided she would never find out! As the knife slid along the refrigerated butter it also slid along the end of my finger and cut off a sizeable chunk including the nail. I was now standing with more than I bargained for in the frying pan and a finger that was spurting volumes of blood. I ended up in the local doctor's surgery with a tetanus injection in my bottom and a very sore finger swathed in bandages up in the air. Since then I've restricted myself to the more pleasurable business of eating the food rather than offering to prepare it.

12

Pride and Joy

I was sitting with Cliff Richard's mother at Wembley Stadium one evening as we watched him perform in concert when she suddenly smiled and said, 'You know, I'm so proud of him.' It struck me how strange it must have felt for her, almost as though she were on the outside looking in. Here was this man she'd given birth to, changed his nappies, now all grown up and filling Wembley on eighteen consecutive nights. Most of the world never thinks of a celebrity as someone's child – it's the secret every mother carries with her, but if she's lucky, now and then she'll get a chance to crow about it.

My oldest son Paul, although he never complained about it, has had a lot to strive for following in the footsteps of his sister, a talented straight-A student who always knew exactly what she wanted. Paul's the first to admit he wasn't academically brilliant. He was also definitely a more laid-back personality than his siblings. Whereas Caron and Michael were always the performers, Paul retained the more reticent demeanor of his father.

Observes Michael: 'There was a time Mum felt a bit concerned for him because Caron and me are terribly outgoing and perhaps Paul felt somewhat intimidated by that. Paul, however, has a wonderful sense of humour. In recent years we've all had more in common. He came down to stay with me and Caron when we were in Wales and brought his friends. We all had a fabulous time.'

Paul agrees. 'I would think I'm not as close as Caron and Michael. Michael's grown up with her more socially and it's a geographical thing, with them both being in London. But we see each other three or four times a month. We've got a lot closer in the past couple of years.'

Even as Paul prepared to sit for his O-levels he was unsure of the direction he was headed in. He harboured visions of being a top session drummer, but during his final year in school he spent a lot of time in the drama department, working with sound and lighting equipment, to the point where his theatre instructor wouldn't stage a production without him. Finally the teacher suggested to Paul, 'Have you ever thought about taking a stage management course? You've got the perfect aptitude for it.'

To be admitted to the Guildford School of Stage and Drama, however, required sitting for A-levels. Displaying a tenacious determination, Paul went in for a two-hour interview and said, 'Look, even if you send me back for A-levels I'm probably not going to pass them anyway, and besides, it would cost you to do that. So why not spend the money to have me take this course?'

Amazingly, Paul succeeded in talking them into it and was awarded a grant to attend the three-year course – incidentally the same year as Michael Ball. At seventeen he showed remarkable maturity, getting a small flat and living on his own in a strange country.

When he graduated jobs weren't all that plentiful but I recall being at a dinner one night and seated next to Jack Tinker, the drama critic. We shared similar stories of our children finding it difficult to land a job. He remembered that Paul wanted to be in the theatre and much to our delight, three weeks later he rang up and suggested Paul get in touch with Paul Farrah, who had a very successful company. How fantastic of him to even remember, never mind do something – and what a turning point it turned out to be.

Farrah was the best teacher Paul could have had and in 1988 he formed his own company, Delta Sound Inc, with his partner Mark Bonner. These days he travels the world doing the sound for theatrical performances, orchestras and conventions. 'If you come from a success-ful family people expect you to be just as successful,' Paul reveals. 'There's pressure to excel, which I think is a good thing. I couldn't stand being the poor brother in the family. For what I've achieved as a man still in his twen-ties I think I'm pretty successful. My business is more than just a job, it's my life. Funnily enough, I've never had aspirations to become a presenter, although coming from a show business family has helped me to deal with celebrities because I have a good understanding of how they think.'

I think every parent will admit it's hardest to let go of the youngest child. Michael and I are especially close because it was 'him and me against the world' those first years in London. He became my closest confidant, which gave him a tremendous amount of maturity because I treated him like an equal. I never excluded him from any-thing. If I was having a dinner party he was always at the table with us. It was never a case of saying 'This is for adults so you have your tea early.' I truly don't know what I would have done without him.

You must have gathered we are a close-knit bunch and never apart too long without contact. So the day Michael came home from school and said he was off with The British Schools Explorers Society on a six-week expedition to Greenland took us by surprise, to say the least. Here was this boy who wouldn't walk the mile to school when he could cadge a lift there and back, contemplating walking across Greenland. Undaunted, we started to get the kit together, and being from a non-military family we consulted a colleague who was formerly with the SAS. He advised us about the survival gear, the Gortex Bivvy bag to keep him dry, the kit bag, medical supplies and so on. The boots he was advised to break in over a period of many weeks, but as I recall, he walked four miles one Saturday to a friend's house and I got the predictable call to come and pick him up – that was the extent of his training.

The plan was that the party would fly to Iceland, be dropped into Greenland by a tiny aircraft in small groups of six and from that moment, they would be totally uncontactable for six weeks. I used to tease Michael that if he saw a helicopter land out of nowhere he'd have a good idea who it was. After much planning and packing the day dawned for his departure. I rushed home to cook him his last proper dinner for six weeks, when I heard a shout from upstairs. Somehow Michael had misread his departure time and we had to rush to the airport there and then. It was like something out of Monty Python. Had he eaten anything, was everything packed in the rucksack, would we make the flight on time? As it turned out Michael couldn't even lift the rucksack into the car, it was so heavy. We all struggled with it and I could not see how he was going to walk hundreds of miles with this thing. It transpired we had packed it all wrong. We had put the heavy stuff in the bottom instead of the top, which made it unbalanced. At the airport I casually asked one of the leaders, 'How far is it to base camp once you land in Greenland?' 'Fourteen hours,' he said nonchalantly at which point I nearly passed out with trepidation.

When we eventually got the call to say he was taking off from Iceland to Greenland I pictured the fourteen-hour struggle. I went to bed thinking about him and when I got up he was still walking. I went to work – he was still walking. I plotted the course in my mind every inch of the way. Later, Michael was to say he would have cheerfully died at any point on that journey. As you would expect, they had the most wonderful and exciting time in this land of the midnight sun and to show how their fitness improved over the six weeks, they ran back into base camp in something like four hours. That expedition was the making of Michael. He came back a well-organised, efficient individual, much more confident in his capabilities. He just loved his welcome home. From the front door upstairs to his bedroom was a trail of goodies starting with soap and talcum powder – as they hadn't really washed in six weeks – followed by treats of all his favourite biscuits, cake and chocolate. He vowed never to eat a Mars bar in one go again, as on the expedition, with limited supplies, they rewarded themselves with a bite of chocolate every five or six miles.

By the way, the hiking boots have been in the roof space ever since.

Michael's goal is to become an entrepreneur – he's always got about nine things on the go. Following in his sister's footsteps he attended Bristol University, where he not only worked for the station, Radio Lollipop, but managed two nightclubs. Upon graduation in 1992 with a degree in English and drama he landed a fabulous opportunity. Caron had been offered a four-month job presenting 'Summer Scene' in Ebbervale, Wales. She'd only been married a year and was keen to have a bit of company at her isolated Welsh cottage. Michael applied for and got a position as a trainee researcher.

'Initially I hated it,' he recalls. 'I was a driver for all the celebrities appearing on the programme. What I quickly found is that people treat you like dirt if you're the driver. When they find you're the brother of the presenter, however, their whole attitude changes. The nicest guest was definitely Sheila Ferguson of the Three Degrees. She insisted on sitting in the front seat, bought some sandwiches, and we had a great chinwag all the way back to London.'

Before long this resilient and ambitious lad eventually became the show's full-time music researcher and found himself inundated with calls from record companies pleading to get their artists on the programme. Through that opportunity Michael went on to do their public relations for both Guild Films and Polygram, the world's largest independent music video producer. These days he's gone totally freelance, and most recently has landed an entertainment spot on LBC, one of London's top radio stations, and is also due to join Caron and me on our Family Affairs programme. Soon all three of us could be in competition with each other!

Michael's very much the peacemaker in our family, displaying the same sensitive quality my mother had. Now and then Caron and I have rip-roaring rows and

Michael inevitably steps in to restore order between what he dubs 'these irrational fiery ladies'. I happened to mention this on air and shortly afterwards I was approached by an elderly woman in a shop who said to me, 'I want to thank your son Michael for something he said.'

'You know Michael?' I asked, confused.

'Well no, but you may remember you mentioned on air that he was something of a peacemaker, and that when things get ruffled he always says, "In the end what does it really matter?" I thought to myself, that's a really good philosophy. In the end, what does it really matter? And that sees me through.'

I walked away thinking how such an innocent comment could really make an impact on someone's life. It gave me a warm feeling of admiration for my son.

What's that saying, a son is a son until he takes a wife, but a daughter is a daughter for the rest of her life. With Caron and me that goes for both of us. We've become more like sisters or best friends. She claims I have more patience, yet she's definitely more laid-back than I am. A few years ago we were doing the children's Royal Variety Show and I was pacing up and down, going over and over my lines to make sure they were in my brain. Caron, meanwhile, was across the road having a hamburger and a beer until five minutes before we went on.

Caron and I have always been exceptionally close to the point of being telepathic. I would instinctively sense when she was ill while away at university and ring her up. One time Caron strongly felt something was wrong and rushed home to find me quite shaken after I'd crashed into a car coming the wrong way down the motorway. When I had my tennis accident Caron was driving over Battersea Bridge when she suddenly felt moved to turn around and head for the studios. When she arrived I was being examined by the doctor.

The first glimmer Caron showed of wanting to be in television happened at about the age of fourteen. I was driving her to school one morning when she suggested a game of 'let's pretend'. 'I'll be an interviewer,' she told me, 'and you be Rod Stewart. C'mon, Mum, you've got the perfect hair for it.'

I went along with the idea and Caron struck right to the heart of things. 'Rod, tell us, why do you dye your hair? What about those leopard-skin tights? And what's the real story behind fetishes for wearing women's underwear?'

Out of the mouths of babes, as they say, though neither of us could possibly guess we were glimpsing the future that day. In fact, the parallels in our respective careers are quite remarkable. At seventeen Caron was hosting a regional programme much like that radio show I did back in Canada. Then came a fateful break that led her to hosting the BBC Belfast youth programme, Channel One. She had just come home from Bristol with every intention of doing documentary research when the presenter of Channel One died suddenly in a car crash. Caron found herself right back in Belfast working with many of the same people she'd grown up with on those long ago tag-alongs with Mum.

Then in 1986 came her monumental break on 'Blue Peter'. Between you and me, there couldn't have been a child more mesmerised than she had been by that legendary show. Caron watched devotedly and wanted to make every project, dumping cereal into the bin to have use of the box. The same with washing-up liquid and egg cartons. Caron would have me running out at a moment's notice to buy pipe cleaners, straws and, of course, that infamous sticky-back paper. You just couldn't live with her unless those requests – nay, demands – weren't properly met.

I had no idea of the show's staggering popularity until the day the 'Blue Peter' presenter Lesley Judd made a public appearance at a Belfast museum. It was a foregone conclusion that Caron had to be there. With Paul in tow the three of us pulled up in front of the museum where the kids were gathering in droves. To my amazement a full complement of twelve security guards surrounded Lesley, making for a scene of absolute bedlam. The children couldn't get anywhere near her. Suddenly I heard one of the mothers cry out, 'Look, it's Gloria Hunniford!' These kids, so disappointed they couldn't get close to Lesley, heard the exultant cry and shuffled en masse towards me.

'Who are you?' they barked and even though they didn't have a clue, demanded I sign autographs. I couldn't believe it. I was being swamped by kids without a security guard in sight. All of a sudden Caron and Paul became separated from me, carried away until I could no longer see them. I was being trampled underfoot by parents and children alike, totally out of hand. 'Caron! Paul!' I cried out hopelessly. At long last, order was restored – in hindsight our first taste of Blue Peter mania.

Caron's big break was no less exciting than my own had been. It marked the first time in 'Blue Peter' history that two of its presenters were female. Accompanying this coup came the inevitable outcries of nepotism. 'Of course, her mother got her in,' or 'Obviously strings were pulled.' But in fact the 'Blue Peter' producers didn't even connect Caron as my daughter, since she used the name Keating.

She further explains: ' 'Blue Peter' wasn't the kind of organisation who were going "Hooray, you've got a famous relative!" In fact, producer Biddy Baxter wasn't looking for that kind of publicity at all, especially since the programme had eight million viewers and had been running for thirty-two years. This business is far too competitive for a producer to take you on because of who your relatives are. If your mother's a famous brain surgeon they're not going to say to you in hospital, 'Hey, come along and be a brain surgeon too. You'd probably be good at it.'

When Caron initially applied for the job she heard nothing for six months. Then one day she got a call from Biddy Baxter informing her of an opening for a presenter – could she come and audition? As hosts on 'Blue Peter' are called on to perform a variety of athletic skills, would-be presenters had to pass certain physical requirements. As it turned out, Caron was given the one sporting thing she was good at, the trampoline, and so duly impressed the producers. With her other sterling qualifications she eventually won the coveted position.

Still, once the story was leaked to the press that the newest 'Blue Peter' presenter was indeed my daughter it became a mad scramble to push up the date of her first appearance.

The first day she appeared on the programme was incredibly exciting. I was doing Sunday Sunday on LWT. We stopped rehearsals and switched all the TV monitors in the studio on to BBC 1. I felt so proud of Caron that day. However, when I learned Caron's assignments were wrought with the perils of motorbike sidecar racing, mountain scaling, and horseback riding with lances, I couldn't help but worry. I'd be calling her every night saying, 'Caron, that looked so dangerous. Should you be doing this?' Little did I know that on one episode she had gone down into the ocean off the coast of California in an underwater cage to film blue sharks. As if that thirty-minute adventure wasn't harrowing enough, in an un-planned manoeuvre Caron actually left the cage to swim to the surface through a menacing school of twelve-foot creatures. I was on holiday in the States while Caron was filming and was in my hotel room watching TV when she phoned to tell me about it. 'It was a very tense time,' she confessed, 'Shut up in that cage I felt like a piece of bait.' Somehow the fact that she was with expert divers didn't do much to allay my alarm. Incidentally the film I was watching when she rang was *Jaws*!

Caron encountered another off-the-wall experience on an earlier show when she had to ride a pack pony into the studio. 'Everything went fine in rehearsal,' she re-members, 'but when we went on the air he wouldn't move. I kept tugging away, urging the pony on, but with no success. Then I looked down and saw he was perform-ing all over the stage, right in front of the cameras. I was so embarrassed. I just sat there horrified.'

Caron quickly learned that being in the spotlight has its pitfalls. She received several hurtful comments about her Northern Irish accent and her wardrobe, and inevit-able comparisons to me.

Caron explains, 'I'd just come from university and didn't have much money and was dressing in clothes from Oxfam. I always thought I'd get to a certain age and turn into this well-groomed and glamorous thing – now I realise I never will.'

Caron was always most individual in her dress sense. We had many a sartorial scrap when she was growing up. I'd be trying to persuade her to get into some pretty pink lacy dress and all she wanted to wear was torn denims with bits of dishcloth wrapped round her wrists and neck. Gilly, our lovely babysitter, was disgusted to learn that Caron dressed from Oxfam. She'd say to Caron, 'You should get your mother to give you more money for clothes.' Of course the kids who watched 'Blue Peter' loved Caron's look, but I'm not so sure about the parents.

Her decision to leave 'Blue Peter' in 1989 was a brave one. To walk away from the pinnacle of children's television was seen by many insiders and the public as an ill-advised move, much as when I had left Ulster Television to do radio. To her credit, though, Caron was determined to sidestep the pitfalls of the entertainment business. So many people are ready to pigeonhole you into one groove, but she wanted to pursue adult programming, to further her professional growth.

It was quite tough going at first but Caron soon emerged as a versatile presenter with such diverse credits as 'Fourth Dimension', the 'Radio One Breakfast Show' plus the arts and entertainment programme 'Wide Angle' for Anglia TV, and the Barcelona Olympic Games. And then in 1992 Caron and I joined forces for a little piece of history. 'Family Affairs' came out of a long-standing mutual desire to work together.

We'd been searching for a joint project simply because it seemed a natural with both of us in this business. Initially we came up with a concept of a celebrity chat show across the generations. We'd book someone like Sean Connery and his actor son Jason, or Christopher Plummer and his actress daughter Amanda, and thereby generate interest from a wide span of age groups. I would relate to the parent, Caron to the child and along the way we'd garner some lively and insightful interchanges. It's an idea I think has merit and one we'd both like eventually to pursue.

In the meantime, however, another premise came up, the more education-based format on BBC 1 where where Caron and I would bring on guests from a wide range of fields, from medicine to athletics to social issues. On one programme, for instance, we discussed the dilemma of working mothers and had as a guest actress Patti Boulaye. She freely admitted she screwed up the early years with her daughter because she was working so hard. At one point she even sent her back to her mother in Africa for a year because she simply could not cope. In the context of that format I was able to ask Caron, 'How did you feel about me as a working mum? Would you have preferred it if I'd stayed at home more?' and thus draw on her own experience, which really gave the programme a uniquely personal touch.

On another programme we brought on Olympic swimmer Duncan Goodhew. He had much adversity in his early life. An accident in the school gym at the age of ten caused his hair to fall out. Then when he was fourteen he was diagnosed as being dyslexic. The show pointed out that all children, no matter what their disability, can excel at something with enough encouragement and dedication.

'Family Affairs' had an initial run of five months in the autumn of 1992 on BBC 1 and we're all set for another five months in 1994. These days Caron has also found her niche as showbiz correspondent for Carlton's London Tonight, so we often end up vying for the same celebrities.

Professional achievements aside, the memories that linger are the personal ones, always falling back to family.

The marriage of your firstborn, especially when it happens to be a daughter, is perhaps the very pinnacle. Caron had her share of boyfriends over the years, one or two I admittedly wasn't wild about, but in the main she was always quite sensible about men. With Russ Lindsay it began the way all solid, lasting relationships should, with a friendship. When Russ became Caron's manager she slowly began to know him better.

Caron picks up the story: 'I invited him to a party to celebrate my birthday. We just clicked that night and realised there was a chemistry and a special attraction. The next day we went out to see a Jean Michael Jarre concert. We both had big grins on our faces because we were so happy together.'

Adds Russ: 'Within a week of meeting Caron I virtually said to myself, "I'm going to marry her." You instinctively know when someone is right. And for me I knew deep down it was only a question of time for us.'

While every mother dreams of a fairytale wedding for her daughter, Caron's superseded my wildest expectations. I wasn't sure anything approaching a conventional wedding would come off, recalling my maverick daughter's staunch declaration to be married in a 'white top hat and tails'. I was therefore inordinately pleased when she decided she'd like a church ceremony in the very traditional month of June. As she wasn't attending any specific church in England she and Russ became parishioners at St Peter's on the Hever Estate, home of the exquisite thirteenth-century castle in the lush Kent countryside.

We spent months sitting around the kitchen table organising the event. The most difficult task was paring down the guest list. Fortunately, we were saved by the small confines of Hever, which could only accommodate some ninety guests. Another problem was the potential media circus the nuptials might attract. Caron was adamant that her wedding be an intimate, memorable affair with only family and friends, and not marred by tabloid reporters bullying each other for photos and quotes. She decided in the end to give *Hello* magazine an exclusive to the story, which in hindsight was the best move she could have made.

Selecting a wedding gown is, I think the highlight for any mother and daughter. We visited a shop on the Old Brompton Road where Caron got into a spectacular bridal dress that was set off by her small waist. As she emerged from the dressing room I burst into tears thinking, my baby's about to become a bride! By the time she tried on the twentieth frock, I was sick to death of the whole thing.

Caron finally decided on the young designer, Phillipa Lepley, who fashioned a breathtaking Victorian gown of white silk with a scalloped v-necked bodice. The painstakingly detailed eyelet-lacing featured a butterfly and intricately woven vines of hearts. Crowning her veil was a delicate silver tiara fit for a princess.

We made a weekend of it. That Friday night all our relatives and friends, many making the trip over from Ireland, booked rooms in the castle, and Caron met cousins from Manchester she'd never seen before. Following a robust party at the Henry the Eighth pub, right on the estate, we returned to our rooms, just Caron, myself and two of her closest mates. We stayed up half the night, engaging in a real girly chat which became something of a pre-wedding confessional. Caron's charming friends confessed up to a few wild going-on that had occurred during university – perhaps better left unsaid till now.

When the girls had gone off to bed, Caron gave me a special gift that just about floored me. Val Doonican, who's remained a close family friend, has a song entitled 'The Special Years' with a touching lyric that goes: 'From pigtails to wedding veils, from pinafore to lace. And in between are the special years that time will never erase.' Caron presented me with a double picture frame: one side contained the photograph of me tying her pigtails with the inscription 'from pigtails to wedding veils'; the other side was empty, waiting to be filled with the photograph of the two of us with the wedding veil. That's when it really hit me: my Caron, my firstborn was about to become a married woman. In a rush of emotions I burst into tears, overcome with it all.

The following morning, 15 June 1991, I was able to turn the tables on her. The entire family burst into Caron's room, tray in hand to serve her breakfast in bed. On the tray was a silver cover under which she assumed were scrambled eggs. 'C'mon, eat your eggs before they get cold,' Don urged. Caron opened the lid to find a velvet box containing a very special surprise, a familiar and cherished diamond ring. The ring was a family heirloom belonging to Don's mother. He'd given it to me but when we split up I didn't feel comfortable keeping it, so I'd returned it to him. As it was supposed to be handed down to Caron, Don and I decided her wedding day was the perfect time to pass it on to her. 'Oh, grandma's ring!' she cried, totally overcome and awash in tears of joy. It had been an ongoing joke over the years, with Caron constantly pressing her father, 'Dad, when am I gonna get the ring? Maybe this Christmas?'

While the men went off to the pub for an all-male brunch we girls did the same, once again taking a final opportunity for a long chat. It was suddenly all rushing by too fast. We were at the final countdown, scurrying about in that heady flurry of excitement that reminded me of a favourite childhood story, Louisa May Alcott's *Little Women*. We were all dashing about getting the make-up on, fussing over our hair, getting the dresses just right.

My spirits immediately fell, though, when I peered outside to see rainclouds hovering ominously overhead, about to ruin our glorious day. Our plans included an open horse-drawn carriage that would take Caron to the church as well as a champagne reception afterwards in the spectacular Italian gardens. I had had visions of Caron floating across the green like a heroine out of a gothic romance, tossing coins in the duplicate Trevy Fountain while guests sipped champagne by the lake and wandered through rose-covered passageways.

Providentially by late afternoon there was just enough of a break in the clouds to allow a bit of sunshine on this joyous occasion. The local people all turned out to watch Caron set off in the elegant black carriage festooned with trailing garlands and drawn by two magnificent white horses, accompanied by her proud father, looking quite dashing himself in his top hat and tails.

As they arrived at St Peter's the medieval atmosphere was set with the lone Scottish piper waiting outside the ancient stone church. Kenneth Turner, a long-time family friend had decorated the church with banks of flowers on the altar and sheaves of bouquets adorning the pews and the proverbial roses round the door of the church. And then Caron was escorted by her father down the aisle, bearing a bridal bouquet of wild roses, lilies and trailing ivy, looking every inch the radiant princess I knew she would. She was given away to a beaming Russ, who looked splendid in full traditional Scottish dress with a kilt of red and green tartan from the Dunfermline-based Lindsay clan. He did break with tradition in one respect: he wore boxer shorts underneath the kilt!

I had anticipated weeping buckets throughout the ceremony but I was apparently all cried out from the emotional weekend. I got choked up thinking back to my own wedding, which made me feel the absence of my parents, but I managed to remain relatively dry-eyed as Caron and Russ marched blissfully arm in arm down the aisle, now husband and wife.

Afterwards the couple were driven by carriage to the drawbridge by the moat for a photo session before making their way into the Inner Hall, where the string quartet who'd played at Buckingham Palace filled the richly carved panelled room with music. Kenneth Turner had also decorated the banquet hall: candelabrums fashioned from birch poles and terracotta planters were all around and fresh strawberries and cherries were dripping over the table.

Afterwards the guests danced the night away to live music in the marquee. Russ made eyes well up all round when he made a touching toast to his new bride: 'I think I have married the most charming, intelligent, elegant and beautiful woman possible. I look forward to a long, long time with you, Caron. It is a dream come true for me. I love you enormously – you're the best thing that has ever happened in my life.'

Most of the guests stayed over that night so it was wonderful to wake up the next morning and continue the festivities. We had a delightful surprise. Caron and Russ had booked a suite in a hotel about twenty minutes away. However, they were so entranced with the castle they had only pretended to leave and instead had snuck into their bedroom through a French window and spent the night there. When they turned up to greet us at breakfast the excitement started up all over again.

When the newlyweds finally departed for their honeymoon in the Seychelles I felt I hadn't lost a daughter at all, but gained a very special son-in-law. I had always worried about Caron's welfare, but from the moment she and Russ became serious, I ceased to worry. He simply looks after her so well.

13

Politics and the Ayatollah

Now that I am living away from Northern Ireland and can look at the political troubles there objectively, it upsets me greatly that all Ulster people are tarred with the one brush. Onlookers assume that ninety-eight per cent of the population are in constant strife with each other when it is actually a minute percentage keeping the troubles going.

After twenty-four years of it, the vast majority of people just want to get on with their lives. I admire so much that Northern Irish resilience which says I won't let the extremists ruin my business or drive me from the country. Of course with thousands of deaths and injuries many families have paid dearly and suffered enormously. I would never want to diminish the extreme devastation in any way. However, in the main, the troubles have been restricted to the ghetto areas like the Catholic Falls and the Protestant Shankhill Roads in Belfast, Londonderry and the border areas between North and South. Strange to think that, to us living in Hillsborough, just fourteen miles from Belfast, there were times when we found it hard to believe that those television pictures of bombings, rioting and shootings were going on such a short distance away.

In the very early days of the troubles, one slogan that slipped the net of the Northern Ireland Tourist Board was 'Come to Ulster for your Shooting Holidays'. Nowadays I hear myself sounding like one of the Tourist Board employees, when I say it is a beautiful country, the people are generally warm and very friendly and there is a great quality of life there – despite the troubles. Perhaps in my area of business it was very evident when trainee reporters were sent to Northern Ireland as part of their training. Three months attached to the Belfast news room was the equivalent to three years' experience in London. The telling part was that a high percentage of them applied to stay on as long-term reporters. They loved the essence of life there, the warmth of the people, the great golf courses, never far away from the sea and easy road access. Of course one has to know certain areas to stay away from and, yes, you can be very unlucky and innocently be in the wrong place at the wrong time.

Caron and Paul were seven and five when the conflict began in 1969. Michael was born in 1970 so they all grew up during the troubles. Ironically the closest Mike has been to a bomb was in Harrods on that tragic day in December 1983 when six people were killed and many injured. Michael and Neagle had gone off to look for sports gear and I stayed on the ground floor. I clearly remember being at the fountain pen department and a call came over for all supervisors to get in touch with management, or words to that effect. It crossed my mind that if I'd been in Northern Ireland I would automatically have assumed it was a bomb scare. I was deeply engrossed in my shopping when suddenly there was that distinctive thud in the ears and the feeling of an earth tremor when the bomb went off.

Thankfully I was in the middle of the store and not on the bomb side. Then came the instructions to leave the building as quickly and efficiently as possible. Instead I was totally panicked – was there another bomb ready to go off and most important of all, where were Michael and Neagle? What I'll never forget was the orderly silence as people filed out of the shop and were ushered as far away as possible around the side streets of Knightsbridge. Yet the silence was pierced occasionally with tears and cries of confusion and panic, particularly from elderly people worried about making it out in time. In the main there was that eerie silence of the stunned.

Outside, every car I went past was a potential time bomb, primed and ready to go. I scurried like a frightened cat back to the safety of my own car, parked a few blocks away. As I turned the corner I fully expected Michael and Neagle to be waiting but they were not there and subsequently I went through the longest and most agonising twenty-five minutes. By now reports of deaths and injuries were spreading like wildfire around the whole area and I became convinced they had been caught up in it. Now it was my time for my tears of worry and fright. By the time they turned the corner I was a total wreck.

It is interesting to witness in a place like Northern Ireland how conditioned people become to bomb scares and the aftermath. Security is naturally extremely tight on a day to day basis, so one accepts it as the norm to be bodily searched along with handbags and shopping. At one stage there was a complete sealed security ring around the main shopping area of Belfast with just a few entry points and long lines of people queueing to go through – a bit like security checks at the airports. In this case, the bags were manually searched and yet again at the entrance to every shop, so it became an inbuilt reflex as you went into a store to open your bag.

Sometimes the security got more than they bargained for, like the friend of mine who worked for the Mastectomy department of cancer research. When they opened her bag of supplies they found a great variety of false boobs which she used for teaching purposes! You can also imagine the stares I got when I first went to London. I would subconsciously go to the nearest official-looking man at the doors and open my bags for inspection.

One of the side effects of the troubles, as our children were growing up, was that we always had to know where they were going at night. As we lived out in the country they had to be picked up or at least assured of a lift home. In a strange sense it probably gave us more control over them as teenagers than we normally would have had. We also encouraged them to bring their friends home as much as they wanted. Better to have them there than at a pub which might be the target for a bomb.

Paul took me at my word and our converted roof space became a rehearsal room for his fledgling rock band. Ever since he was a tot, Paul aimed to be Buddy Rich and in the end had a drum kit Buddy would have been proud to play. He would wash cars and run errands to finance the next cymbal or snare drum. For birthday and Christmas presents we were well instructed in advance, so in the end Paul was surrounded by all the equipment he had ever dreamt of. The band rehearsed in our loft for what seemed like years. They called themselves 'Santa Cruz' and I seem to remember a long line of girl singers who had to audition – at least, that was Paul's story! The audition piece was Fleetwood Mac's 'Dreams' and Caron was most affronted because she was not allowed to try out, even though she was word perfect. Eventually she persuaded Paul to let her audition, and it came as no surprise that she didn't get the job.

After the rehearsals, there were the gigs, and as I drove Paul and all his equipment to the various venues, I found myself wishing he had taken up the flute. Paul eventually went on to other things, but Vivian Campbell, the lead guitarist of Santa Cruz, went on to play with Thin Lizzie, White Snake and Def Leppard, and I often wondered if he ever thought back to the streams of tea and coffee in my roof space.

Although I loved my work with celebrities I harboured a secret desire to sink my teeth into some really hard news. After all, I'd originally come to London on the strength of my work with Good Evening Ulster, a current affairs programme.

Fortunately, the old instincts were very much intact as I tackled heavyweight issues from perestroika to green politics to the Strangeways Prison riot in the BBC 1 series 'Gloria Live,' which replaced 'Kilroy'. What we wanted was to go behind the headlines to offer politics to viewers on a palatable level.

I never worked so hard in my life. We'd take on four major topics every day. The reading I had to do overnight was phenomenal! It really made me appreciate what the breakfast television people had to go through on a daily basis.

My schedule was the most gruelling I'd ever undertaken. I would get up at 4:30 and by 6:30 arrive at Lime Grove Studios for a production meeting with my editor, Charles Miller, along with the producer and researchers. After an hour and a half of make-up and rehearsals, 'Gloria Live' went on the air. Afterwards I'd have a canteen breakfast with the production team about the next day's show. By 11:30 I would arrive at Broadcasting House in search of a quiet corner to read through the research for my Radio Two show. Following my two hours on air I would practically collapse with a cup of tea and a sandwich. I then set off once again to Lime Grove, this time for a 'Gloria Live' evening production meeting where we discussed each item for the show and decided on a line of questioning. It would be eight or nine before I'd get home, only to pore over my notes for the next day and fall into bed to do it all over again the following morning.

My social life was non-existent and it was clearly a pace I could only maintain for those six weeks. The experience, however, really stretched me and provided the stimulating challenge of pursuing world issues. One of the highlights for me was meeting Helen Sharman, Britain's first female astronaut. I remember the childlike thrill of just wanting to touch her, this woman who'd been in space. She had been a scientist working for Wall's ice cream when she heard a radio ad proclaiming: 'Astronaut wanted'. She applied for, and eventually won the position, beating out some 15,000 applicants.

It was a Soviet venture and she travelled to Russia for eighteen months to train and learn the language. Helen has a wonderful knack of reducing her adventure to basics that anyone could comprehend. I was fascinated as she revealed how she could not only locate Britain from space, but pick out motorways and rivers simply by the naked eye.

The format for 'Gloria Live' changed for each of the series. After the initial six-week run focusing on politics, the second series softened to include two serious topics and two lighter ones. The final chapter in 1992 proved an innovative platform for a theme-based programme.

We did one show on danger, another on the history of food, and we also dealt with parent-child relationships. The latter was most enlightening. Viewers discovered that MP Ken Livingstone was given an old-fashioned dressing down by his mother who was still angry he had refused an invitation to Princess Diana's wedding, presumably because that meant she didn't get to attend. Glamorous weathergirl Ulrika Jonsson confessed she hadn't ever forgiven her mother for walking out on the family.

The day to day grind of 'Gloria Live' aside, the public wasn't at all prepared for what hit them on February 19, 1992, with controversial author Salman Rushdie and I going toe-to-toe on live television. It was hands down, the most challenging interview of my career.

I'd been standing in for Terry Wogan that week while he was away on holiday when one morning my producer said to me, 'We've been offered an interview with Salman Rushdie, live.'

To say this was a white hot exclusive was an understatement. The author of the explosive *Satanic Verses* in hiding from assassins for over three years, did the occasional recorded interview and surfaced now and then for an unannounced literary luncheon. But this was the first occasion he agreed to appear for a live television broadcast. There were only three people in the BBC, the editor, producer and myself who were aware of this historic coup.

The security detail for this event was naturally of the highest level. Special forces scouted the area in advance to discern the quickest route to the studio. Sharpshooters were posted at strategic points throughout Television Centre. On the evening of his arrival, Rushdie, under escort of a Special Branch guard, was ushered into the building just minutes before the programme and left immediately afterwards.

I researched this story like no other. What I knew about Rushdie was simply what I had read in the papers. I scoured every known source for one and a half days. What I discovered was an overwhelming pro-Rushdie attitude in the name of free press and speech. On the surface he certainly appeared the victim. After all, no one could condone the Ayatollah Khomeini's pronunciation of the death sentence, the fatwa, on someone for putting out a literary work, no matter if it did somehow offend the Moslems.

There were unanswered questions, however, such as his continued round-the-clock protection from Scotland Yard at the taxpayer's expense. And what about his former wife, American novelist Marianne Wiggins, who denounced Rushdie as a weak, self-obsessed man who failed to campaign for other writers who were prisoners of conscience? I therefore made a very conscious decision to play 'devil's advocate', to ask the really tough questions, knowing that once I forged down that controversial road there would be no turning back.

Salman came out on to the set, expecting, I've no doubt, another cosy, sympathetic chat. I began the conversation by asking what it had been like in hiding and having to re-locate dozens and dozens of times. In Wales alone, he'd made twenty-nine moves in only a few weeks.

Then I moved up a gear. 'You realise, of course, your protection is costing a million pounds per year. I'm sure the average taxpayer would wonder why should we pay for Salman Rushdie's protection?'

He went off on a tangent saying, 'If Terry had been here I was going to remind him of the time I used to write television commercials for him.'

On one hand, he was telling me he'd had enough of hiding, that the fatwa had been enforced too long, that he didn't mean to cause any offence.

'Given all that,' I said, 'are you still planning to re-lease the paperback, considering you've already made six million pounds on the hardcover version.'

He puffed up and said, 'Of course I am!'

'Well, you'll only reiterate the offence,' I told him. 'You're going to drag it all up again.'

'But that is my right. The principle hasn't changed. For three years people have been lying about me and say-ing terrible things, that I did it all on purpose.'

'The argument is that it was all calculated to sell books.'

'Every author's work is calculated,' he replied. 'But when it comes to satire, should you sentence the creator of *Spitting Image* to death? For three years I've had to hear people blaming the victim. I do not take responsibility for my own murder.'

Then I really tore in, referring to political comments that the affair might have delayed the release of the hos-tages in Beirut.

'That's a terrible thing to say,' he snapped. 'I've been a hostage to the hostages. I haven't been chained to a radiator, but I've been hunted by killers. The danger is not a joke. I am not to blame. I am not prepared to go into hiding any more. We will fight against it and we will win. I see my future as returning as a serious writer.'

As soon as Rushdie, in a furious huff, was whisked out of the studio, the switchboard was flooded with calls from viewers. It was a mix of praise and condemnation. One viewer, an accountant from Bedford said, 'I felt Gloria was quite vicious, she was pillorying him. Even her facial expressions were aggressive.'

A friend of Caron's though, probably summed it up best: 'I was sitting at home idly reading the paper with one ear to the television when all of a sudden I heard that Salman Rushdie was on live. I went to the edge of the settee to look on and suddenly there was your mother, normally this sweet, affable person going after it like a bull terrier!'

The next day it was all the buzz round London. Not only did the public seem shocked at my aggressive stance, but the papers made it headline news. One reported: 'Miss Hunniford subjected the author of *Satanic Verses* to an astonishingly tough inquisition. At one point, with an uncharacteristically fierce expression on her face, she attacked his motive for writing the book. To think Gloria was uncharitably described in this page not long ago as being like the ever-smiling senior stewardess of an island-hopping Celtic airline. An injustice to be sure!'

The ramifications were far-reaching. Rushdie went on BBC Radio Four's 'Woman's Hour' where presenter, Jenni Murray questioned him about his personal responsibility for the predicament. He retorted. 'For three years I have been vilified to a degree that few human beings ever are by everybody from the Ayatollah Khomeini to Gloria

Hunniford!' Everyone at the station absolutely loved it. I'm sure that's the one and only time my name has ever been linked with the Ayatollah. At the end of my stand-in stint the team gave me a blown-up version of the newspaper cutting, which is proudly displayed on the wall at home.

Looking back over my career the most memorable moments have been the unexpected ones. Like the time I came into the studio to do my radio show, same as always. Five minutes before air the engineer bursts in with the announcement, 'I'm sorry, but the whole studio bank has gone down. You're gonna have to move studio.'

This meant moving all my notes, dedications, records and setting up again. I just made it to the microphone to hastily blurt out my opening and go into the first record. I told the engineer, 'You know, that microphone sounds very odd to me.'

'Oh no. It's just the record,' he assured me.

I went to another record and once again complained about the sound. This time he came in and said, 'Let's have a look at that needle' and proceeded to lift it right off the record in the middle of a song.

'Hey, you berk,' I erupted, 'this is going out live. Put it back on the track!' He slammed it down with a crash and I thought, what in heaven is going on here? I knew this engineer was something of a mad hatter anyway and by the tanned look of him I figured the sun must have got to his brain.

We're in the middle of another record and he stomps in and says, 'That still sounds like crap to me.' He lifted the needle off once again, took off the record and to my horror, broke the thing over his knee.

My jaw dropped to the floor, convinced the guy had

totally flipped. My face contorted in anger, I glared at my producer, incensed that he was doing nothing to bail me out of this. Meanwhile, I opened the microphone and tried to be as calm as possible. 'Believe it or not, something really odd is going on in the studio. This guy, an absolute nutcase, came in here, took the record off and broke it in two. I don't know why, but oh well, here's Elton John . . . and he can break this one too if he wants.

Off air my face was drawn and rigid with fury. No one was coming to my rescue, leaving me to try and do a professional job in the midst of chaos unconfined.

All of a sudden in strides none other than Noel Edmonds and his film crew with that familiar refrain, 'Gotcha!'

Gullible as I am, I'd become another victim of the infamous television prankster. I'd had absolutely no clue. My relief was immense when I found out I was not going out live at all, but a stand-by programme had been airing all the while. They'd rigged it, and when I peered into the cubicle there was a huge box marked 'technical equipment' in which was housed a cameraman with a full-sized camera. They had also removed the speakers from the wall and put hidden cameras in the studio.

In the midst of my heated embarrassment I vowed to Edmonds, 'I'm going to get you for this if it's the last thing I do.'

I made good my promise. In conjunction with Noel's producer I set up my revenge around the popular segment of the show called 'Wait'll I Get You Home' where the child talks candidly about his parents. Thanks to our ruse, this child turned out to be a little more outspoken than usual.

On the show that night the little boy said, 'Oh, my Mum's name for my Dad is Mr Tubby because he's so fat.'

In the studio, the parents were not amused. The husband said to his wife, 'Look, I don't think this is funny. Nobody said they were going to be insulting.'

Meanwhile, the zingers kept flying and the husband was getting thoroughly riled as the wife frantically tried to calm him down. Finally the irate father stomps up to Noel and rails, 'This is appalling! You get parents here under false pretences. You make our children say these terrible, intimate things. I'm totally disgusted and offended. I've got a top job in this city and how am I ever going to show my face in the office after this?'

A red-faced Noel immediately stopped the recording. 'I never intended any of this,' he began to apologise profusely. 'I honestly don't want to embarrass you and certainly didn't get you here under false pretences. If you don't want it to go out, it won't.'

In the middle of all this, the announcement rang out, 'Now here's your son!' Instead of the boy, out I walk, my face beaming with satisfaction. 'Gotcha!' I fired. Noel's face was priceless, totally stunned. The plan was brilliant, for things were not at all as they seemed. The 'family' was, in fact, actors one and all, including the boy, hired by Noel's producer. I'm sure their performance warranted an Academy Award in Noel's mind!

If you happen to be in the right place at the right time you can land a real coup. In the late eighties we took the radio programme to the States, presenting Christmas in New York. Before we left, a record company rang up asking, 'Would you like to do an interview with Yoko Ono while you're there?'

It was almost a rhetorical question, so far fetched was the probability of the legendary Yoko granting us an interview. When we landed in New York we got a call telling us to go to the Dakota Building. On arrival we were ushered upstairs through the triple doors to Yoko's apartment. We found ourselves in the much publicised white room, with the grand piano made so vividly memorable in the John Lennon 'Imagine' video. We were left there for forty-five minutes and served tea by Yoko's oriental maid. It gave us a great opportunity to nose around. The airy room contained glass furniture, lush green plants and dark tapestries in contrast to the white walls and plush white carpeting. Yoko's chair went against the pattern of the room, facing towards the breathtaking New York skyline. She told us that was where she conducted her business calls. There were all the family photos proudly displayed along with the brass plate on the piano bearing the inscription 'To Yoko, Happy Birthday. This Morning A White Piano.'

She came in, a diminutive figure with flawless porcelain skin, to give a charming interview. She pointed out a unique dish hanging on a wall. 'One night we were having chocolate ice cream in the white dish. After we finished, John dipped his finger in the dish and wrote "John Loves Yoko". The next morning it had hardened and I thought the pattern so lovely I had it sprayed to preserve it and hung it on the wall.' Simplicity against opulence.

14

Wear and Tear

It never fails to amaze me how obsessed the public are with women's appearance on television. Jan Leeming probably had more publicity about her earring falling off during the news than she ever did about the quality of her news reading. Who could forget the furore over Angela Rippon showing her legs. Male broadcasters just have to worry about a clean shirt and a different tie, a quick comb of the hair and they're off. Women do have the concern about their clothes – do I have the right jewellery, must I go to the hairdressers and so on.

I recall one lady coming up to me in the street and saying 'Every Sunday when you're on the telly, I get down on my hands and knees in front of the TV set and get a closer look at what shoes you're wearing.'

Cynthia Payne or 'Madame Cyn' put in her book that one of her old boys used to come alive when he saw my black stockings and high heels every Sunday.

Dressing for television can be quite an art unless you're the perfect size ten. First of all, television adds about ten pounds in weight to your appearance, so I now know pretty well what to wear to try to 'skim down.' Out are voluminous dresses with masses of material, particularly in the sleeves – that only makes you look broad right across the bust and shoulder line. The less material the better all round for a trimmer look. For me, classically tailored suits with padded shoulders give a nice clean-cut simple line. Square shoulders make the remainder, particularly round the middle, look slimmer.

The outline of the hair is also very important as any photographer will tell you. Patrick Lichfield once explained that whereas make-up, clothes, etc. are all part of the image, hair is the single most important thing for the overall shape. I get teased about the number of times I go to the hairdressers each week – I virtually live in John Freida's in South Audley Street in London. I have very straight hair and simply cannot manage it after washing, without the professional twist of the brush. I don't suppose I have washed my hair at home more than a dozen times in the last ten years. I know that's very extravagant, but it is all part of the job. If I can't get to the salon, Tracy or Jane will come to the studio. I haven't seen my true colour of hair since I was about seventeen, so I've made the girls promise if I'm ever unfortunate enough to be marooned in hospital for a long time, they'll come and do the colour for me – I don't want to grow grey on the pillow.

The kids used to say my hair is how they used to find me in supermarkets – they would look for the shock of blonde hair above the stacks of food. I suppose it's become something of a trademark.

I also get teased unmercifully about putting on lipstick all the time, even on radio. My producer will say 'It's only radio' but I always imagine my mouth works better with plenty of lipstick being added throughout the programme.

I want to be buried with my lipstick and my shoulder pads – just in case!

When I've been interviewing glamorous women on television, it can be a bit of a nightmare as to what to wear. There is no way I can match up and yet I don't want to appear dowdy by comparison. Joan Collins, a few years back, was the first guest on a new series of Sunday Sunday. A journalist asked me what I would be wearing opposite the extremely glam Joan. At the time I said 'I'm not sure, I'll probably dress down.'

Off the show's designer and I went and as a real treat we bought a beautifully cut Emmanuelle dress, simple with a flattering line and a deep band of ruched black satin at the bottom, complete with a sassy bow at the back. I felt really good as I took to the air, which also helped my overall confidence. Joan came on, looking wonderful as always, in a swathed fuschia pink number – I did the intro and welcome and Joan started 'Good to see you again, Gloria. I see you've dressed down for the occasion.' People always ask how Joan looks close up and the answer is fabulous. She has been blessed with great skin and I believe her when she says she hasn't been under the surgeon's knife. She believes it's in the genes because her father Joe, in his eighties, would have passed for twenty years younger. Joan has done so much for the older woman and compared to any age group, always looks sensational.

All of us at LWT found out the cost of always having to look sensational. Raquel Welch spend a record 'four hours' in make up before the show. She then demanded to be already seated on the set when the interview started and we had to explain that everyone must make a walking entrance. She then spent ages deciding how she was going to walk out, where she would sit, and which was her best side. In her defence, Raquel has an exact eye for detail and in a throwback to the old style of Hollywood, dedicates herself to giving the public the best she can. However, I felt she was so obsessed by how she looked she didn't really relax and give a good interview. Whereas when she came on the radio programme, she was a totally different person – affable and a fund of good anecdotes.

Friends always say, 'Where do you get the energy?' But this is aided and abetted by a daily intake of vitamins. I got to know Jan de Vries through Radio 2, and he proved to be one of the most popular men in broadcasting. He's a qualified homoeopathic doctor, an osteopath, an acupuncturist and has studied aromotherapy. He is a very balanced, measured man who is totally dedicated to his profession but sensibly regards his treatments as complimentary to orthodox medicine as opposed to alternative. From time to time he works out a routine programme for a busy schedule. So here's how I rattle to work each day.

Urticalcin . . . For bones and to prevent osteoporosis.

Oil of Evening Primrose . . . A great internal healer and fabulous for skin.

Ch 3's – available in good health stores and what Barbara Cartland calls her brain pill . . . It's a multi vitamin tablet and great for energy.

Immunostrength . . . For the immune system.

High dosage of vitamin C which Jan says is the most important of all to keep colds and flus at bay and sometimes extra dosage of vitamin A & B.

I know the general medical profession will say, if you have a good diet you don't need vitamin supplements, but my eating pattern is very erratic and sometimes not good food at that, so I reckon as long as I'm sensible, these vitamins can do nothing but good.

I also pay regular visits to Joseph Corvo, the renowned zone therapist. Quite simply his theory is to do with the energy air waves which flow through our bodies. He says if you can keep these from clogging up, then all the organs will work much more efficiently. Jo manipulates certain pressure points on the feet and face and has sold his books and videos on the theory worldwide. I usually go for general well being, but in recent times, I've had a bit of calcification on a joint in my foot which Jo has been manipulating with those healing hands of his. He has often had patients referred to him from eminent doctors who feel they can't do anything more for certain patients, so in a way he's regarded as something of a miracle man.

Friends are often sceptical at the beginning when I recommend these natural treatments, but when the chips are down, they are usually pleasantly surprised. Of course I'm not saying they work all the time, but I'm dedicated to the subject and what I'm pleased about more than anything, is that at last, the orthodox medical profession is now giving a little more credence to the subject.

I'm not a great one for exercising. With the exception of tennis I've never been great at all those physical jerks. Last year I decided I would indulge in some one-to-one training which would motivate me in the right direction. I hired Derek Evans, who at that time was partner and trainer to Tessa Sanderson, the Olympic athlete. Derek is black and mean when it comes to 'doing it'. So three times a week at eight o'clock he would arrive at my house in Sevenoaks, get the funky music going and for an hour he'd crack the whip on stepping and exercising all parts of the body. Normally I would do them in the garden and heaven knows what the commuters passing our gate en route to the station must have thought, when they heard him shout 'Do it woman, just do it' . . .

Sometimes when I was slaving away on the exercise bike, we would talk about applying his skills to television, and as you may know he is the latest sensation to hit breakfast telly as 'Mr Motivator'. I'm very pleased for him and predict a great future for him in this country. I know he will be very amused to learn that I'm involved in making a video on health and fitness. This will be the perfect anecdote to the usual supermodel variety on the market. I think the average person looks at some of these and thinks 'If I worked to doomsday, I'd never look like this.' So the one I'm making along with Lydia Campbell will look at the possibility of trimming off seven pounds or thereabouts and deal as well with all round health. I know my own family think it's hysterical and so will my tennis friends Libby Lees and Carolla Bird . . . they know all about my stamina!

On the subject of energy, my friends often inquire 'Why do you work so hard?' The simple truth is I love it and feel very fortunate to have a job which I look forward to each day. There is always a new set of people to meet and different topics to cover. I'm always relieved when my controller, Frances Line, comes round and offers another contract for the following year. I adore radio as a medium. The pictures are always best on radio and I can always weave my little fantasies about being in the fishnet stockings and suspenders or the little satin number slit to the thighs. Listeners often ask if Ed Stuart and I really dislike each other, because we say 'terrible things' to each other on the handover at the end of the programme. The truth of the matter is I rarely see Ed – he's in one studio and I'm in another – but it is all in fun. If we really hated each other, we wouldn't say the things we do on air.

Being the one up front you tend to get all the kudos, but really the programme would never get on air every day without the team who work so hard behind the scenes. Researchers like Caroline and Camilla, who painstakingly research each celebrity from our news cuttings library. Secretaries like Val and Alison, who become friends with our regular listeners and offer a ready reckoner service with all sorts of queries, ranging from when is Neil Diamond in concert next, to what benefits can I get as a 'carer' in my own home. At the moment my production team is led by Gary Bones with Alison Tuoey and occasional visits from Dennis O'Keefe, whom we laughingly call 'the old faded film star'.

It's this building up of images in the mind of the listener which makes radio so popular. Most people have access to a radio whether it's on the road, in a combine harvester, or sitting on a beach. I've had listeners say our programme is played in the milking parlour, because 'It calms the cows down', and office workers who tell me they hide the radio in their desk drawer – every day away from the boss. I love the intimacy of this one-to-one relationship over the air waves. At least I don't have to worry about the hairstyle on the radio.

Broadcasting may be my first love, but for sheer adrenalin you can't beat a live performance on stage. I think my greatest challenge in that respect came when Roy Heybeard, artistic director of the Arts Theatre, Belfast, asked me to do 'Side by Side by Sondheim.' Ned Sherrin, Millicent Martin, Julia Mackenzie and David Kernan had made a wonderful success with it in the West End and on Broadway – now it was the turn of Belfast. Anyone who knows the complexity of Sondheim's lyrics will know that two and a half weeks to learn that show is an almost impossible task, particularly alongside a daily television programme. I played the record so much that in the end Caron knew all the lyrics before I did. I will always be grateful for those hours and hours in her bedroom when she acted as prompter. I am sure she really wanted to get on with her own projects but she told me on opening night how proud she was that I got through it. At least I knew that if I collapsed I had the perfect stand-in.

Barry Cowan, my BBC television colleague, was the narrator and the other singers were Candy Devine from Downtown Radio in Northern Ireland and Liam McQuillan who had been a great success in many of the Arts Theatre productions. Both Candy and Liam have wonderful voices, so it was a great challenge to keep up, and also my first experience professionally of being directed for the stage. Roy did a very dramatic and sophisticated interpretation of the show and I was determined to have the dress to go with it: a black velvet backless number with a split right up the front and a very luscious pink feather boa used to great effect in the number 'I Never Do Anything Twice'. This song became very much an in-joke because when we decided, on the strength of our two-week success in Belfast, to take it to Londonderry – only four people turned up. We never did get the chance of doing it twice. Obviously Derry wasn't ready for us!

15

Tinsel & Tiaras

Through my work with various charities I've been fortunate enough to rub elbows with the royal family who, of course, are patrons of many worthy causes. My association, however, hasn't always run a smooth course. It actually began rather dubiously back in Northern Ireland when I was presenting 'Good Evening Ulster'. We were covering the presentation of the Duke of Edinburgh Awards at Buckingham Palace and had arranged an interview with the Duke himself. I was simply awestruck walking down those hallowed corridors with the prospect of conducting the interview in the historic Green Study where Queen Elizabeth delivers her annual Christmas address. Before Prince Philip arrived I suddenly decided I'd better go to the loo and make sure I looked my best. The Queen's loo was just down the corridor and I hurried off in great anticipation, thinking, this is as close to the throne as you'll ever get!

As I was leaving the loo one of the footmen came up to me and warned, 'I'm sorry, Ma'am, but you'll have to get into the room. The Queen is coming along with the corgies.' No visitor could be seen in the corridors in the presence of Her Majesty – a tradition to help protect her privacy.

Another time I was invited to a coffee morning for the Heart and Lung Foundation. There were only twelve of us chosen, the idea being to promote the event in the hope that everyone else would go off and have coffee mornings of their own. As part of the official ceremony I was requested to help Princess Diana and a patient who'd undergone a heart and lung transplant cut the cake. As we placed our hands on the knife I quipped to Diana, 'I think this means we're married now.' That drew an immediate laugh and I felt quite good about our moment.

Sitting around afterwards in a less formal atmosphere, along with Patricia Hodge and Jane Asher, the conversation turned to our children and the stories they'd written for school. Diana said she had been mortified when William wrote about his Granny having 'lots of castles with soldiers marching up and down outside.'

I thought it quite amusing. That was, until the next time I met up with the Princess of Wales in a receiving line. She looked at me coolly and said, 'Oh yes, you must be the one who gave the story about William and his stories to the press.'

Immediately taken aback I replied, 'Sorry, Ma'am, not guilty.' I didn't waste a moment of time but quickly got hold of her press secretary and said, 'Look, you've got to put the record straight. I did not give the press that story.' In fact a member of the Foundation had innocently related it to a reporter. That incident, however, will be forever remembered as the day I got told off by Princess Diana.

Of course, it could have been much worse. That same day the Princess of Wales accompanied Dr Malcolm Green, the Foundation's organiser, to a hotel complex in Bristol that featured the first smoke-free bedrooms. I was asked to say a few words and again managed to put my foot in it. 'I'm surprised the tabloid press isn't here,' I said, looking out on to the gathering, 'to find out why Princess Diana and Dr Green were locked away in a bedroom in Bristol!' Diana roared with laughter.

I don't know what it is, but I always seem to manage to draw attention to myself in the midst of the royal family. In October 1992 Princess Diana was holding a private reception at Kensington Palace in conjunction with the hospice movement in which she and the Duchess of Norfolk are heavily involved. As I had done some work with the movement I was invited along with others from all over the country.

The reception was held in an impressive wood-panelled chamber boasting highly polished floors with connecting doors to the Princess's private apartments at the far end. Diana, looking as elegant as ever, circled the room, taking the opportunity to speak to everyone present about the hospice movement.

Finally, the Duchess of Norfolk stepped on to the podium and announced that the Princess wished to speak to the workers and thank them for their efforts. As the Duchess began her introduction, all of a sudden I heard a loud *Beep, Beep*. I was in the first row of the gathering and thought with annoyance, My God, it sounds like someone's phone battery going down.

Beep! Beep! Now it had claimed everyone's attention, sounding like a loud roar in the hushed room. Security was instantly scouring the crowd while Diana was looking very nervous. A man I'd been chatting with earlier had wound his way from the back of the room to the front and urgently whispered, 'Gloria, your handbag is ringing!'

In a moment of thoroughly wretched embarrassment I realised it was true. Awkwardly I slunk through the gathering towards the back of the room. Eyes followed me with a mix of indignation and disdain as I tried to look nonchalant. I found myself grovelling on the floor to open my handbag where the ring now bellowed like a foghorn – hardly standard behaviour in the presence of royals.

I'll never forget the night of the Queen's Fortieth Jubilee celebration, 26 October 1992. The Royal Opera House of Covent Garden had been recreated inside the massive Earl's Court. On hand was a one hundred piece orchestra and a choir of five hundred to launch the royal pageant. The enormous hydraulic-powered stage boasted a trackway through which the coronation coach, one hundred and fifty members of the Royal Household Cavalry, plus vintage cars all paraded. All the top sport celebrities from forty years showed up, including Arthur Ashe and the World Cup tennis team of 1966. Cilla Black, Cliff Richard and Michael Ball were just a few of the entertainment luminaries on hand. The Majors and the Thatchers, plus other politicians of note were also guests at this unprecedented gala.

Afterwards, the 5,000 guests were invited on stage to participate in an informal party with the royal family. I couldn't believe what I was seeing. True enough, my invitation had read: 'The royal family will mingle with the guests', but I had given little credence to it. After all, such a thing simply was not done, had never been done in this country.

On stage the royals were fourteen strong, strolling about, chatting with the guests: Queen Elizabeth and Prince Philip, Charles and Diana, Andrew, Edward plus Princess Michael of Kent, Princess Alexandra, Angus Ogilvy. Protocol dictates you should speak to the royals only when they approach you. I didn't get the opportunity actually to chat with them, but star-gazer that I am I was content just to breathe in the spectacle. To see the Queen in her blue chiffon gown with diamonds and sapphires sparkling from her tiara just three feet away was thrill enough.

Following this fabulous evening, my escort and I walked out into a typical London drizzle to discover our car was nowhere to be found. We strode up and down the street, searching for the missing chauffeur for a good forty minutes, my elegant full-length coat and dress getting thoroughly soaked. Eventually we gave up the search and I had to stay the night with my friend. The car had all my belongings in it: my cases, jewellery, my clothes for the next day, all my scripts.

I showed up at Television Centre at half-past eight the next morning in my crumpled evening frock. I looked for all the world like a dirty stop-out. I discovered our chauffeur had been locked in a special car park and couldn't go in or out due to heavy security. They had allegedly been ferrying people back via minibuses, but no one had bothered to tell us of the change in plan. I must say I know of more romantic ways to round off an otherwise magical evening.

I always cite Cliff Richard as the most consistently terrific guest to have on any programme. You could ask him about anything – the wall, cosmetic surgery, South Africa, holidays – and he would have an opinion on the subject. He is a consummate conversationalist and one of those rare individuals who could chat about a bread box and make it sound fascinating.

I first met Cliff in 1970 during my stint on 'Good Morning Ulster'. Cliff was in town to perform a religious concert in LIsburn where I was living at the time. Very few celebrities would come to Northern Ireland because of the troubles and the news was that Cliff was definitely not giving any interviews. My rule of thumb is that you never get anything if you don't ask so, undeterred, I went to see the local vicar and asked 'Is there any chance he'll give me an interview?' The vicar replied, 'I gather not but I'll tell you what, give me your number and I'll make representation for you.'

To my amazement I received a message to be at a certain address at six o'clock and bring my tape recorder with me. I was ushered into the library and after a few minutes in came Cliff. 'This is Miss Hunniford' said the vicar whereupon I lumbered cumbersomely out of my chair, an enormous eight months pregnant. Cliff smiled warmly, clasped my hand and proceeded to give me the most captivating interview. I got a lot of brownie points back at our office for landing an exclusive with this pop music icon.

We always seem to have a great deal to chat about and I'm proud to consider him a friend. We're the same age, we love tennis, vitamins, lotions and potions, and we share a great interest in gardening. Every year we go to one of the big flower festivals like Hampton Court to decide what we might plant in our garden next. Mind you, I only have half an acre compared to his eight. His gardens are kept in stunning form by his gardener Mick Bateman, an endearing man who always sends me off with a basket of fruit or flowers. A couple of years ago Cliff decided to clear out a portion of 'the woods' to create a kind of enchanted forest. He has picnic and barbecue areas and has incorporated a sound and lighting system in the woods. I even got him a tape of sound effects for night time and it's quite fun to hear cheetah cries, elephant calls and bird songs. To inaugurate this latest venture he threw a woodland party to which all the guests came in costume as characters from the wood. It was like a scene out of a movie with a pig roasting on the spit and all these wonderful creatures milling about. There were Red Riding Hoods, Maid Marions, Big Bad Wolves and Cliff himself, who cut a dashing figure as Robin Hood. I foraged through a costume shop to come up with a cloak of chiffon leaves called 'the tree spirit'. The only problem was that an evening spent tramping through the woods left me with a bare trunk and all my leaves stripped off!

This year the theme was Country and Western and Cliff and his manager Bill Latham emerged as the Lone Ranger and Tonto. It's always fun to see this legendary star in ridiculous clothing having such a relaxing time.

Last time I saw Cliff at Wembley he invited me to join the gang for dinner afterwards. As we drove out of the backstage area I was amazed at the hundreds of people who just wanted to touch the car. If only they'd known – we were only going round the corner to the local Chinese! The same thing happened a few nights later when Princess Anne asked to see the show along with Tim Rice and party. Once again Cliff wined and dined Princess Anne on Chinese food. I imagined if royalty were going to a local restaurant in Wembley it would be closed off for the night. Cliff remembers one eager chap who said on his way out, 'Cliff, fab concert. Never expected to see you in here, mate.' Apparently Princess Anne adored the anonymity.

The other subject which is a favourite talking point of ours is vitamins. Cliff wouldn't let a day go by without his usual quota of vitamin A, C, cod liver oil and kelp for healthy hair. On one occasion nutritional expert Leslie Kenton sent a package of skin tablets to Cliff, care of me. I took them over to his house and said, 'Are you really going to take these? I know nothing about them. He practically snatched the package from me and beamed, 'Are you kidding? Of course I will. As long as it doesn't do me any harm I'll take anything that will do me some good. On air one day on Radio 2 I asked him if he would have cosmetic surgery when the time was right. 'No doubt about it,' he replied. 'I want to be like Cher and have whatever nips and tucks necessary.' Next day all the papers were full of shots of Cher with Cliff's head superimposed on her body. He enjoyed that one.

I think he also enjoyed our night of 'passion' but in this case it was passion for rock and roll at the opening of 'Good Rockin' Tonight', a Bill Kenwright production about the life of Jack Good, who had discovered for television Cliff, Marty Wilde, Adam Faith, etc. It was a fabulous opening night with 'the real celebrity names' joining their characters on stage at the end of the show. At the party afterwards we happened to be with Cliff and his group and inevitably when the music started up we took to the dance floor. Though I say it myself we're a good pair of jivers and we really went for it. The press photographers could hardly believe their luck, seeing Cliff so off guard and having fun. We danced the night away, only to open the papers next morning to headlines like 'Wrinklies Show the Young 'Uns how to do it' and 'Rock around the Crock'.

Su Pollard is another star I'm proud to call a pal. When people see us together it's like 'what's wrong with this picture?' We do seem the ultimate odd couple, this straight-laced miss conventionally paired with the scatty, hyperkinetic Hi-di-hi girl. One day I was having tea in the very reserved Langham Hilton and in blew Su. 'Hello Glo! Hi doll! Say, what ya think about my wig?' and proceeded to whip it off her head, sending the room into fits of laughter.

I love her exuberance, this constant exhilarating whirlwind of energy. Yet underneath that facade lies a very sweet, caring personality. One day she came down with then husband Peter Keogh for a Sevenoaks barbecue. She was immediately taken with my mother and spent the entire day playing matchmaker between Mum and our charming neighbour, John Baker. Once Su gets a glass of wine into her there's no controlling her. She'd call over the fence, 'John, May's here, why don't you come across?' Then, to my mother, 'Well, May, looks like we'll have to team you up with John next door. We've gotta fix you up with a man, May.' She even talked John into giving Mum a couple of yellow roses. 'Look here, May, John's proposing to you, you've got to give in.' I can still hear Mum laughing.

Afterwards when Mum was in hospital Su sent her flowers, cards, notes, the kind of gestures you never forget. That's the kind of generous heart she has.

Su tells a hilarious story about her wedding. When she found her future in-laws couldn't make the ceremony in England Su decided, in effect, to bring the mountain to Mohammed. On a pre-marriage visit to Australia she locked herself in the plane's miniscule toilet and dressed in full bridal regalia. Upon landing Su burst on to the ramp, fairly tripping over her gown, arms flung wide and bellowed, 'Hello Mum! Hi Dad! We're married!' to the stunned and amused looks of passengers and waiting families.

Though subsequently divorced, Su still comes over to the house for birthdays and celebrations or to spend the odd weekend. She routinely shows up in some outrageous get-up; one in particular remains etched in my mind, when she came with two odd shoes, madcap earrings and a collection of coloured glasses. By the time she goes home I tell her to her face, 'We're worn out, we're breathless.'

She was in utter convulsions of laughter when she arrived at my fiftieth birthday. Once again I had hired a room at Hever Castle near where we live in Sevenoaks. So Su had been doing cabaret but had promised to arrive come what may. She picks up the story . . . 'Ooh Glo, I was dropped off in the car park, was dying to go to the loo and decided to crouch down behind this car. Well I was in full flow, Glo, when suddenly the car moved off.'

Which reminds me of another friend, Kay Kennedy, a very accomplished journalist in Northern Ireland, who wanted to go out on exercise with the army when they first arrived in Northern Ireland. The Colonel of this particular regiment was a little reluctant to take a woman out all day and when it came to Kay needing to spend a penny he said 'I've organised latrines for the men but nothing I'm afraid for you. You'll just have to go behind the bush.' As Kay was in full flight, to her horror the bush moved off.

Val Doonican is one of the most entertaining people I've met. He has that gentle Irish way of weaving in and out of a story and he has certainly been blessed with the gift of the gab. Our paths have crossed many times since my broadcasting career began in Northern Ireland. My first encounter was way back in my early days at UTV when Val used to sing on tea time programmes with his wife Lynn. Once, after recording an interview for the World Service at his home, he gave me a signed print of one of his paintings which hangs in my hall at Sevenoaks as a much valued possession.

Val would always say to me 'Why don't you have a go across the water – I think you'd do well in London.' Little did I think at the time I would ever make the leap. So when I settled in Radio 2, Val gave me my first national TV spot. His Saturday night programmes went out live – in itself that was pretty daunting considering I hadn't been singing on a regular basis for some years – and here I was complete with a full orchestra, trying not to let Val down. I had this wonderful gun-metal grey, heavily beaded dress which had been made for me as part of a UTV documentary by Sara Percival, so I was OK for the frock, but for some strange reason I ended up letting a friend of mine do my hair for the show. To have the luxury of the huge orchestra was superb – after my little trio at best in Northern Ireland, but I was really worried about hitting the right key amid this very full sound. I decided on a lovely song, 'I Wish you Love', which was pretty safe and I managed to get through it. Then I had to make my way across the studio to where Val was waiting for the traditional duet. Unknown to me some of my precious bugle beads from the dress had fallen off on the set and as I tried to glide elegantly across to Val, I almost went on my ear on the floor. A little hot and flustered I arrived with Val to sing Janis Ian's 'Other Side of the Sun' – it had almost been the other side of me on show to the British public. However one look into Val's kind face told me everything would be alright.

On another occasion some four years later Val was to ask me to perform another duet during a Royal Variety performance, which I was terribly thrilled at. The idea was that within the finale of the show England, Scotland, Wales and Ireland would be represented. Our song was called 'This Land is My Land' and my whole family were out front waiting patiently for my bit to come. Val came on stage and, as they thought, was mostly through the song, but all the time they were wondering where I was – had I fainted with nerves backstage, was I sick – what? Eventually according to plan I came on and joined Val halfway through the song and much to their relief I had made another Royal Variety notch.

All our careers are made up of people who help us along the way and I often bless Val for his wonderful generosity, particularly at the beginning of my time in London, which led to many other opportunities.

I also put Terry Wogan – or the Grandfather as I call him – in that category. He is undoubtedly one of the most amiable and helpful people I have ever worked alongside. Since those initial Radio 2 days of Grievous Bodily Hunniford and Gus Hunnybun we've had our moments. The first year Children in Need transferred to television, the producer decided Tel and I should do a duet, so we opted for Sonny and Cher's hit 'I Got you Babe'. We both donned the wigs, me with the long flowing black hair and five pounds of black eyelashes on my lids and Tel with his sideburns and gringo moustache and the Sonny gear.

Before the show I was actually standing with Su Pollard for five minutes before she realised who it was. What fun we had on air that night and a piece of video which haunted us for a number of years afterwards. It's amazing the things that people will do to raise money for charity.

The British public are unbelievably generous when it comes to donating money and each year Radio 2 kicks off the Children In Need proceedings with twenty-four hours of non-stop fund raising. Neil Diamond is my stalwart each year and is very long suffering when I literally take the clothes off his back to be auctioned for thousands of pounds. Last year his manager said 'Gloria, will you wait until he has finished the tour otherwise he won't have anything left for stage.' The first year his exotic beaded shirt raised over £4,000 which he was very pleased with, so each time he comes across to Britain he always packs what he calls 'his Gloria shirt'.

Last year we had this wild idea to try and rope in a mega name to co-present my section of the programme and on a whim one afternoon I contacted Michael Crawford in Los Angeles. Although Michael has pretty well done everything else, he had never presented a programme and after his initial apprehension he kindly agreed to come over for a couple of days. He joined me in the Children in Need studio pulling those wonderful 'Some Mothers Do 'Ave 'Em' faces and after a few nerves he took to it like a duck to water – so much so I could hardly get a word in.

Every year I look forward to the opportunity just to watch the parade of stars dropping in throughout the day with pledges and merchandise. In 1988 Paul McCartney came by with some items to auction off. Earlier in the week he had gone into a recording studio to record a specially written number called 'What About the Children' with a line-up that included heavyweights Bill Wyman, Ronnie Wood, Boy George and Chris de Burgh. I was so thrilled to see him that in my enthusiastic zeal I grabbed him about the neck, practically strangling him.

Not long afterwards I received a phone call at the station. 'Paul McCartney rang up,' said my producer. 'He's calling back at noon and wants to speak with you.'

'Oh yeah, sure,' I brushed it off, taking it as a joke.

At noon on the dot, Paul came on the line. 'Hello Gloria,' he greeted. 'I just wanted to tell you how much I enjoy the show.'

'Well, thank you,' I beamed. 'I'm so delighted you listen.'

'I wanted to clear up an inaccuracy you had on the air the other day though,' he said. He went on to bring up an article in one of the papers I'd read on air regarding a scene in his 1984 movie, *Give My Regards to Broad Street*. The story reported that in a busking sequence passers-by threw money into Paul's hat as he played his guitar on the street. The payoff line read: 'And guess what, McCartney kept the money!'

'That simply was not true,' Paul said emphatically. 'I'd really like you to put that straight.'

Although I might have come off with a bit of a dressing-down, I was quite impressed with Paul's personal touch for detail, the fact that he took the time to call himself to set the record straight.

I've also interviewed his wife Linda a couple of times, once about her photography, the second time for her vegetarian cookery book, which became one of the biggest selling cookbooks in British history. Linda and I got to talking about our children and it seemed her oldest daughter Heather and my son Michael shared a common interest in pottery. 'Well, you must come down to the house sometime and have a look at our kiln,' Linda suggested and even gave me her home number in Sussex.

Strangely enough, I could never bring myself to ring her up. I don't know what it was, but I just couldn't lift the phone and say, 'Oh hi, Linda, remember you said Michael and I could come down and see your kiln? How about this weekend?'

Because of my father's interest in magic, my own intrigue for the subject has never waned and therefore Paul Daniels makes a perfect dinner guest. He enjoys doing his tricks so much that he always comes armed with a few hidden about his person. His close up 'card' work at the table is superb. There's no problem worrying about keeping the conversation flowing. Few people can top Paul at the clever quips and most are utterly fascinated by his brilliant sleight of hand. On one surprise birthday party which had been organised for me on board one of the long boats at Little Venice in London, Paul stood at the exit at the end of the night and gave everybody their watches back.

During his TV specials, Paul often includes guests passing through, taking part in various illusions. He asked me to participate in a jungle scene. Debbie, his lovely wife, and he were the white hunters and I knew that somewhere along the line I was to end up in the big black pot, do a switch with Paul and make my grand entrance. I thought, here's my big chance to be a magic assistant at last. It was only when I got to the studios I realised I was to be put inside a gorilla outfit, a huge rotund one at that – bang goes the hairdo! The suit was hot and heavy and I could hardly move in this thing, never mind climb up a ladder to hide inside the pot. I was in my crouched position for what seemed hours under the hot TV studio lights, praying for my word cue, so that I could jump out and get the damned thing over with. Unfortunately for me, the camera work didn't go according to plan and I could hear the floor manager shouting to set the studio up again. Panic – I thought, they've forgotten about me, plus I couldn't give away the trick to the studio audience in advance, by coming up for air. By the time they got going once more and got to my big entrance, I was expiring with heat and lack of air. I was almost at the iron lung stage. When I whipped off the gorilla's head there stood this little head on top of a huge gorilla's body, hair wringing wet and looking an utter fright. Afterwards I said, 'Thanks Paul, but I'll ring *you* next time.'

My perfect dinner party would also include the actor Victor Spinetti, who has this wonderful knack of virtually doing his one man show of anecdotes without ever seeming to dominate the dinner party. He is also so graphic in the telling of the story, often getting up and acting out the scenario.

'Darling, I remember Marlene Dietrich when we were walking along the Champs Elysees and she said, 'Look at the traffic, it's like rubies going up and diamonds coming down'. He tells wonderful stories about his friendship with the Beatles, including one when John Lennon offered Brian Jones of the Rolling Stones some Beecham Powders to cure his headache. 'Thanks, man,' said Brian as he sniffed it up his nose. Victor joined us one evening after the theatre for dinner. We had been to see Sharon Gless of Cagney and Lacey fame in the play 'Misery'. On Radio Two I meet people on air and say goodbye on air, so chemistry which leads to a friendship has to be instant. I formed an instant friendship with Sharon.

She had gained two stones for the part on stage which Cathy Bates played in the movie. When she came to the studio I hardly recognised her, bearing in mind we had shared a Royal Variety dressing room the year before. I could barely hide my reaction. Gone was the size ten figure with short blonde hair and instead here was this overweight actress, no make-up, long dark hair scraped back from her face. She said even she didn't recognise herself in the mirror any more. Her husband, Barney, left this streamlined wife eight weeks before Christmas for rehearsals and when he returned for the holiday season with his daughters he was stunned. Sharon, in a good-natured way, took up the story reminding him he had married her for 'her' and not just looks, a battle which would continue. At the end Barney couldn't wait to get her to a fat farm. He booked her in for six weeks of relentless reducing.

One of my favourite memories of them before they headed back to Malibu Beach where they live, was one evening at Kensington Palace with Her Majesty the Queen Mother as hostess. It was in aid of Brinsworth House at Twickenham, a beautiful home for retired variety performers. Great friends on the committee, Peter Elliott, Laurie Mansfield and Greg Smith had asked me to reply on behalf of Brinsworth to thank the Queen Mum for her hospitality. I started off saying how thrilled we were to be in such magnificent surroundings and how pleased we were that the facilities had been made so graciously available. 'In other words, Your Majesty, in showbiz lingo, thank you for the use of the hall.'

On that evening Dame Vera Lynn sang all the Queen Mum's favourites – 'We'll Meet Again', 'You'll Never Know', 'White Cliffs of Dover' – and my lasting memory will be of the Queen Mum singing along with Dame Vera, word perfect and having a wonderful time.

Sharon and Barney stood at a vantage point watching the events and knowing how much Americans in particular love brushes with our royals, that evening for her was the highlight of her four months in London.

I got myself into terrible trouble live on Radio Two one day. I'd just interviewed the actor Gene Wilder about the film 'Woman in Red'. We'd had a fun conversation in and out of some of the music associated with his various movies, including 'Willy Wonka and the Chocolate Factory'. I finally thanked him and went to a piece of music and then to the news bulletin. I turned to look into the control room and behind the glass Gene Wilder was practically on the floor roaring with laughter alongside the rest of the production team.

They informed me I had just said, 'That was a track from Gene Wilder's ''Willy Wanker and the Chocolate Factory'. Quite a few people rang in to our duty office, but I assured them it was just my Ulster accent!

In the same vein, one of my first producers when I came to London, Brian Stephens, remembers my enthusiasm while on a live outside broadcast from Blackpool. We were doing an interview about 'the mighty organ' at the Blackpool Tower and I was heard to say: 'Ooh, I can't believe it – this takes me right back to Belfast when my Dad would take me to the Ritz cinema and we would see Stanley Wyllie on that rainbow organ rising from the floor. Well, here I am, sitting on Phil Kelsall's organ. It's coming up higher and higher. I wish you could see it – his hands are going all over the place.'

In my professional singing days in the sixties, I was thrilled to be asked to open a concert for the great tenor Joseph Locke, whose story was portrayed in the film *Hear My Song*. The concert was being held in the Grove Cinema, a huge venue by any standard, on the Shore Road in Belfast. I was keyed up and ready for this gig which had received a lot of publicity as Joseph hadn't given a concert in Belfast for some considerable time. As fate would have it, I got caught in a terrible snow storm and was much delayed in getting to the theatre, so the star of the show had to go ahead and open himself. I arrived in a state of total anxiety and I'll never forget what this man of great stature did. He broke off in the middle of his act, explained the circumstances and brought me on, asking the audience to give me extra appreciation for finally making it through.

Some thirty years later, in the 1992 Royal Variety Show, I had the enormous pleasure of introducing Joseph Locke. I had to introduce him as a surprise just for Princess Diana, a huge fan. Backstage Joe and I were chatting and he said, 'This is going to be my last performance. I'm getting too old at seventy-five for this "performing lark".'

So I said, 'If you mean that, why don't you announce that your farewell performance is for Princess Diana?'

He did and there wasn't a dry eye in the house.

16

Envoi

I guess some people will find it extremely odd that, as part of my job, I interview guests about their personal as well as their professional lives and yet never talk about my own 'love life'. Sure, there have been many tabloid articles – but based on the proverbial 'a close friend said' rather than the real story. The fact is that when Don and I agreed to divorce we also agreed never to talk about it to the press. When I am interviewing I always try to assess in advance if the guests mind divulging all, or word the question so that if they say they don't like to talk about it, then I can easily back off. However, there are many people who seem to find it therapeutic to talk publicly about their love relationships, and that's fair enough. Personally I like to keep what goes on behind closed doors within the family, and anyway I am not a kiss-and-tell person.

Strangely enough, I think if I had continued to live in Northern Ireland Don and I probably wouldn't have got divorced; but our circumstances and lives changed, which contributed to it very much. During our twenty-one years of married life we had never at any one time been apart more than twelve days but, as fate would have it, just as I went to London to grasp my big network opportunity Don, for the first time in his career, was offered a production job in South Africa for four months. Caron and Paul were already at university and college in Bristol and Guildford, and as I packed to head to London with Michael Don was off to Cape Town. So as events were to turn out there wasn't the usual splitting up and moving out process. At the time, it was a more natural procedure for job reasons. The rest was a gradual process of circumstances.

I am not a great believer in the idea that absence makes the heart grow fonder; I genuinely feel a relationship has to be fed. But what I am pleased about is that Don and I have managed to remain extremely close – we talk regularly on the phone, and when he comes across to London to see the children we can all go out for dinner as a family unit which remains very tightly knit. I know this has helped Caron, Paul and Michael to see that we genuinely like and have a mutual respect for each other, but I suppose in the end no one knows the full impact of divorce. I remember my lawyer, Monty Raphael, giving me a bit of advice when he was dealing with the divorce. He said: 'Remember you can't put a lid on twenty-one years – there will always be births, deaths and marriages to deal with.'

Don still lives in our family house in Hillsborough in County Down and when I have paid visits there in recent years I find it a very bitter-sweet experience. Trees and shrubs which I planted are now huge and overgrown, the furnishings that we put together are largely the same, each piece of furniture and china bringing back its own memory – where it was bought, what we paid for it and maybe the restoration that had to be carried out. It's like a time-warp, complete with ghosts of life with our children, friends and the community where we lived as a family, and there are times I wish I could whizz the hands of the clock back to experience the day-to-day feel of what it was like all those years ago. I suppose we all feel like that on occasions, irrespective of the circumstances.

I now feel as if I'm in 'the third phase' of my life. It's like being a teenager again. The children have all left university and so on and are settled in their jobs – I feel totally fulfilled in what I do, and I must admit live life to the full. I have never really had to be on my own at any time in my life, having gone from secure family upbringing to marriage at an early age and straight into other relationships. So at times it's a learning process.

If there's one thing to have been gained by a divorce, it's that I have talked to the children about emotions – I have confided in them much more than I ever would have done under normal circumstances. Any time I seek Caron's advice about my romances she good-humouredly says, 'Mother, isn't this the wrong way round? Aren't you supposed to be giving *me* the advice?' Michael does make me laugh when I come home late and he's at the bottom of the stairs with an eye on his watch, chastising, 'Mum – what time do you call this?'

What also becomes reinforced after a divorce is the value of friendships and people whose opinion you trust. For example, one of the first people I met when I came to BBC London was Jackie Gill, a record and events promoter who subsequently became like part of my family. When the chips were down she was always there for a chat, and even now, hardly a day goes by without a tele-phoen call from her.

I do feel women score in this area, in that they are able to talk a lot about emotions, whereas men tend to bottle things up and because of the 'macho' thing don't open up to each other about personal feelings. I know that, irrespective of my situation, my friendships will never be neglected.

Since my divorce I have had a long-lasting and very good relationship of eight years with a Harley Street con-sultant, Neagle Cathcart, which for various reasons didn't work out; and currently I am in another. But the time isn't right for me to talk about either of them – perhaps another story for another day. In a strange way I feel quite excited about what this new period of freedom will bring – a feel-ing of not knowing who or what is around the corner. Health permitting, I feel as if there are so many exciting challenges on all levels ahead, and with whom I am not exactly sure – but, who knows, that may be volume 2.